THE ESSENTIAL CROCK POT COOKBOOK FOR TWO

The Beginner's Step-By-Step Guide to Mastering Crockpot Cooking. 1500+ Days of Easy and Delicious Recipes. PLUS, a Time-Saving Meal Plan and a BONUS Chapter!

By
Luisa Hamilton

Table of Contents

Introduction

Are you always occupied with something and on the move? Do you find making time in your schedule challenging to prepare meals for yourself or your family? Utilizing a crock pot is the solution that you have been searching for. Although you may think of slow cooking as a technique best used in the cooler months, using a crock pot throughout the year may help you save time and provide you with the flexibility to do other tasks while preparing your meals.

You may start the cooking process before going to work using a crock pot, and when you get home from work, you'll have a dinner that's already been cooked and is still warm and tasty. Knowing you'll be coming home to a dinner you made yourself will make it more challenging to give in to the desire to grab something to eat on the way home from work at a restaurant or drive-through window. In the long run, this will save you money and have positive repercussions for your health and waistline.

The food in a marinade will taste better after being allowed to rest for longer, and in the same way, slow cooking will bring out the natural taste of the components. Because the crock pot allows all of the ingredients to simmer together at low heat, they can better take on the tastes of the other components.

Moreover, after the dinner has been prepared in a crockpot, there will be just one pot for you to clean up and put away. Who wouldn't want a little bit less of a mess?

Since this book contains easy, delicious and healthy recipes for two people, the question arises as to why you would get another one, given that this is the only book of its kind. This book provides readers with recipes prepared using a crockpot daily for a whole year. All the recipes in this book are designed specifically for a home with two people.

You now have in front of you the book that is both the most comprehensive and the least expensive. You now have a choice between the following two options: You have the option of continuing to look for other books on Amazon that are both less comprehensive and more expensive, or you can get started right away and enjoy this crockpot cookbook for two that is the most comprehensive one that is currently available on the market.

This book will teach you everything about crock pots. After reading this book, you'll be able to use the crockpot without confusion. It will teach you how to use it, what to cook, how to clean it and much more. You'll also get easy crock pot recipes and meal plans in this book. So, let's get started.

Chapter 1: What Is a Crockpot & What You Need to Know?

As their names imply, slow cookers are cooking machines in which the food is prepared over an extended period. They are the antithesis of pressure cookers, often used because of their reputation for rapidly cooking food. Crock pots are another name for slow cookers. This is due to the ceramic crock often found inside most slow cookers. It is possible to use these for as little as an hour or as much as ten hours, depending on the food being prepared.

1.1 What Is a Crockpot & How to Use it?

It is a pot that may be used instead of a traditional stovetop to simmer meals. This type of pot is also known as a slow cooker. The slow cooker has a high & low setting and an AC connection, but it does not include temperature controls other than a high and a low setting. This is because the temperature of this pot gradually raises throughout a lengthy cooking time and then shuts off by itself. Because it is intended to cook without the need for constant supervision, you may start the cooking process in the morning before going to work, and when you return home about 7 to 10 hours later, you will have a dinner that is adequately prepared.

The pot contents are cooked in foil or baking bags, where the lid does not need to be removed, and the food does not need stirring while it cooks. This will cause the heat to dissipate, resulting in the food taking far longer to cook. Dishes that include seafood are the lone exception to this guideline. During the final 30 minutes of cooking, stir the contents if you are using fish or shellfish that have not been cooked. If the fish has already been cooked, you should stir it during the final few minutes.

You can choose between two roasting times: the standard roast will take around 10 to 12 hours on a low setting or 6 to 8 hours on a high setting. Near the end of the cooking procedure, you may check the internal temperature of the meat using a thermometer explicitly designed for use with meat. Temperatures for beef and pork should register between 160 and 170 degrees F, while those for poultry should reach about 180 degrees F. When adding meat to the pot, you don't have to brown it first, but you may pre-cook especially fatty cuts of meat to eliminate some extra fat. Browning the meat is not required, but it is recommended.

If you want to include pasta in the dish, you should prepare it according to the standard method of cooking it in water that is quickly boiling until it is half cooked, and then add it to the crock pot for the last thirty minutes of the cooking time.

Although the crock pot is most often used to prepare meat dishes, it is possible to prepare vegetarian meals. Preparing a meal that takes about 15 to 30 minutes in a slow cooker will take around 1 to 2 hours on a high setting and about 4 to 6 hours on a low setting in a crock pot. Similarly, if it takes about 1.5 to 2 hours, you should cook it in a crock pot for about 3 to 4 hours on a high setting and then for 6 to 8 hours on a low setting.

It is easy to prepare recipes based on meat that includes hog, chicken, fish, lamb, and a variety of other meats. Cooking curries, beans, veggies, pulses and even soups are all examples of vegetarian cuisine that can be prepared in the crockpot.

Be careful to maintain the veggies in their natural, chunky form to preserve their structure. When preparing food in a crock pot, always use one-third less water than you usually would. Dairy products, rice, pasta and other delicate vegetables should not be cooked in a slow cooker because they cook too rapidly and may become mushy. Also, avoid putting any delicate vegetables in the slow cooker. The addition of dairy products might cause the mixture to become curdled. Ensure that you only add the dairy in the final 30 to 40 minutes of cooking if the meal is based on dairy products.

When you get home from a long day at work, your food will be waiting for you in the crock pot, piping hot, bursting with aroma and flavor, and prepared exactly how you like it. This is made possible because this pot is a fantastic and safe method of cooking meals without direct supervision.

Adding the components of your dish into the crock pot and setting it to the appropriate setting are the only things left for you to do. You may also allow your meal to simmer in it overnight or program it to cook throughout the day while you are at work. Because it can cook food at a low temperature for an extended period, it is safe to leave it alone.

1.2 Who Should Buy a Crockpot?

Crock pots are an excellent appliance if you have to be at work at an ungodly hour and don't have time to prepare meals before you leave. You only need to program it before bed, and your breakfast will be ready when you wake up. These pots are particularly helpful for those who need more time to prepare lunch on their own. You can start the cooking process as early in the morning as possible by adding all the ingredients to the pot and programming it to produce the ideal meal until lunchtime. The food absorbs most of the flavors and aromas throughout the many hours of cooking, another benefit of the process.

1.3 Things to Know Before Using a Crockpot

So, you did it. You've decided to invest in a crock pot and have finally made the purchase! Now comes the point when you open the box, take one look at all the buttons, and start getting anxious about what's about to happen. But now there's nothing to worry about; you can find all the needed information here.

No Manual Button

One of the most notable distinctions between the widely used instant pot and the more recent crock pot is that the latter does not feature a button for manually inputting the amount of time the food should be cooked for. Instead, you have to choose the preset that sets to a time closest to what you desire.

Choose the steam button, for instance, if you want to steam something for ten minutes while applying pressure to cook it. The functions of each button for pressure cooking are precisely the same. It's only that their minimum and maximum time frames, as well as their default pressure settings, are different. Beans and chili are a fan-favorite starting point. Once you have become used to using your crock pot, you will have no trouble selecting the appropriate settings and determining the appropriate cooking time.

Frozen Food

It may seem impossible, yet it is possible to prepare food that has been frozen solid. However, you must know that it will take longer to come under pressure if the food inside is cold or frozen. This is something you need to keep in mind. However, the time it takes to cook can be kept the same, the additional time spent warming up kickstarts the cooking process. Thus the total amount of time required is the same.

Thick pieces of meat need more cooking time; as a result, add a few extra minutes to the total cooking time, but only a little. You should do your best to prepare meats that have been recently thawed wherever feasible.

Although cooking from frozen may be helpful in an emergency, the resulting meat tends to be flavorless and watery since there is no practical method to season meat that has been frozen solid. However, cooking from frozen can save time. It works pretty well with chicken breasts, especially if you're also making some form of soup at the same time.

Weird Noises

As the pressure increases, it gives some strange sounds. If you pay attention to the sound of the steam departing the pot since it alerts you that the next phase of the cooking process is about to start. It's a nifty little gadget that tells you how much longer you have to complete other things and keeps track of the time.

Heating Time

The time required to heat the dish is separate from the total time. On average, it takes roughly ten minutes to achieve the pressure in a crock pot before the cooking cycle begins. When you are cooking on your own without following a recipe, you need to prepare for the time it will take for the food to cook the whole time and the time it will take for the pressure to release.

Cooking Time

While the cooking cycle is in progress, you cannot adjust the cooking time. After selecting it and pressing the Start or Stop button, you are committed to the selected cooking time. The only method to change the time is to press the Start or Stop button again,

which temporarily pauses the process. After that, you can choose a new button and make time adjustments from that point on.

You only need to open the top, let off the pressure, and do a quick inspection to determine whether or not the food is ready. If more cooking time is required, re-cover it and begin the procedure again. The fact that both the crock pot and the food are hot, to begin with, means that it will take less time for the system to get back up to temperature and resume building pressure.

Bobber Valve

You no longer have to worry about whether this valve is in the up or down position, in contrast to older stovetop pressure cookers. When the pressure within the pot reaches a certain level, the lid will automatically lock itself into place. After the cooking cycle has been completed, the steam will begin to naturally release, and after about ten minutes, you will hear a little "click" as the valve returns to its original position. This dislodges the lid, allowing you to open it up once again.

Do not attempt to see through the hole to determine whether or not it is becoming bigger or smaller. Just put your faith in the

procedure. However, food particles may become caught up there and can screw things up, so if you have problems, try cleaning it out with a little tool. This will help if you are having difficulty.

Understanding Acronyms

As soon as you start browsing the internet for recipes or looking for groups on Facebook, you will start coming across a few acronyms. It simplifies conversing and writing down recipes, but it may be overwhelming and challenging for first-time users. So, here are some of the most frequent ones:

- **Natural Pressure Release (NPR):** It only indicates that after the cooking cycle has finished, it should be allowed to release pressure in a usual manner via the bobber valve. After the food has finished cooking, this will begin by itself automatically. The system will bring itself down to temperature on its own time. After the cooking process is finished, there should be around ten minutes before the steam release tab on the valve should be moved to the "Release" position using a kitchen item. Once steam stops pouring from the valve and the lid can be opened easily with just a little effort, the pressure has been successfully released. After this point, you may safely remove the cover and start serving the dish.

- **Pot in Pot (PIP) Cooking Method:** Food is prepared in a separate bowl and then positioned on a steam rack inside the crock pot. The pressure that is built up from the liquid underneath the steam rack causes steam to be produced, which is then utilized for cooking the food. Any dish that can be cooked in an oven and fit within the casserole without touching the sides or preventing the lid from closing securely may be used. This works well for sweets, cooking numerous items at once, and recipes that don't call for liquid.

- **Quick Pressure Release (QPR):** Immediately after the cooking cycle is complete, use a kitchen implement to move the tab on the steam release valve to the "Release" position. The steam release valve will quickly let out its contents of stored steam. Cooking components that include liquid, such as casseroles, stocks, and soups, should never be done using this approach. Rice is notorious for being very fragile. Thus you should never cook it using this technique. Once steam stops pouring from the valve and the lid can be opened easily with just a little effort, the pressure has been successfully released.

- **CPE** stands for Crock Pot Express.

Steam Release Valve

Even though it makes little sense, this valve is meant to remain unattached and be able to move around freely. As you flip it to closed, it will effortlessly move between open and closed positions and settle into the slot when you do so. It is necessary to move it a little bit to know whether it is completely secured.

If this does not occur, steam will begin to escape as the pot attempts to rise to pressure. Over time, it will consume all the liquid therein, and you will get an E6 error code. Around 85 percent of the E6 codes that people inquire about are caused by the valve not being closed correctly or left open all the way.

Food particles have the potential to be blasted up into the valve if a rapid pressure release is performed when cooking starchy foods like stews, rice, or soups. For this reason, you should avoid performing a quick pressure release during these types of cooking. Then, the next time you attempt to cook, the lid won't shut correctly, and you'll continue getting E6 signals, or it won't come to pressure. If this occurs, clean it well and clear it out by running water and vinegar through it.

Condensation Cup

To begin, it is attached by sliding it on. It took me an absurd amount of time to figure out what was going on there. Don't attempt to pry it open by pulling down on it. Move it so that it's not touching the pot. Then you should rinse it as required.

Recipes

The recipes for the Instant pot may be converted to the Crockpot format. When you are just beginning, it is beneficial to have a recipe that will instruct you step by step on precisely which button to hit and when to do so. There are just two things that you need to be aware of: the button that you select for the cooking time will rely on how long you would like to cook, and the non-stick pot rather than stainless steel means that you cannot shred, meld, or stir without using plastic, wooden, or silicone utensils.

1.4 Difference Between Slow Cookers & Crockpots

They are essential to the success of our soups, stews, and quick meals on weeknights. They can even be used to bake bread, in addition to helping to make tough meat softer. We also use their names interchangeably, with the presumption that slow cookers and crockpots are the same things. On the other hand, that is not entirely correct.

Crock pots and other slow cookers prepare food over low, moist heat for an extended time. Both are used to prepare identical dishes, and the outcomes of cooking with either are equally delicious. These fantastic, space-saving kitchen equipment have the same three elements inside them:

- Heating element
- Pot
- Glass cover

On the other hand, they are not the same thing at all! The following is the most productive way to consider: The Crockpot is a kind of slow cooker named after the brand that bears the same name. However, a slow cooker does not always refer to a crockpot.

When it was first released to the public in 1970, the Crock-Pot was first positioned in the market as a bean cooker. Throughout its existence, it underwent several modifications that led to the formation of the version we are familiar with today. Slow cookers similar to the pot are manufactured by many businesses and are, unsurprisingly, quite popular throughout the US.

Branding

The crockpot was the first slow cooker to be manufactured in this style. It is also the brand name of the slow cookers produced by rival manufacturing companies, although many

other brands sell slow cookers in the Crockpot style. They are built with a ceramic

or porcelain pot placed within the heating unit. Slow cookers of this sort may heat the food from both the bottom and sides of the pot. However, this is only the case for some of them. The container may also be oval or circular and is available in various sizes.

Most Crock pots have just two heat settings: low wattage, which raises the temperature to somewhere in the region of 200 degrees F, and high wattage, which raises the temperature to somewhere in the range of 300 degrees F. Some models additionally provide a third warming option that has a lesser wattage.

Cooking

Crock pots continue to cook food even after the power is turned off. A timer is included on specific versions so that the food may be cooked for a predetermined time. There are other slow cookers designed for commercial use, which differ significantly from Crock pots and others in several respects.

Marketing

The slow cooker is not a brand name; it is merely a generic term for the cooking device. A large number of different companies produce other varieties of slow cookers.

Construction

Some slow cookers feature a metal pot that rests on the heating unit. The bottom of the pot is where all of the heat comes from. Because the heat is focused at the bottom of the pot, the food could take longer to cook than it would in a Crockpot. Additionally, there is a more significant risk that the food will burn on the bottom, and you will need to stir it more often. Due to the increased stirring, the lid must be opened more often, which causes heat to escape and causes the cooking time to increase.

Most slow cookers of this kind come with several different heat settings in addition to the traditional low, hot, and warm options. The majority have at least five different temperature settings.

These slow cookers with bottom heating may operate in cycles during the cooking process, turning on and off the power supply. A timer is included on specific versions so that the food may be cooked for a predetermined time.

Most items on the market that are branded as "slow cookers" contain the characteristics of a Crockpot-style slow cooker, which includes a ceramic bowl that is put within the heating unit and both low and high heat settings. This is the primary cause of misunderstanding.

When searching for and purchasing a slow cooker, the bottom-heated, more commercial-style machine discussed before is one of many things that spring to mind for us as customers. Instead, it is a slow cooker in the form of a Crockpot branded as a "slow cooker."

You are free to utilize any when it comes to the kitchen. There is one feature that all slow cookers, regardless of brand or design, share: they all simmer food at a low temperature, and they perform all of the work while you are absent.

Chapter 2: How to Choose a Crock Pot?

A Crockpot has become an indispensable appliance for today's busy home chefs. Because you can use cheaper pieces of meat in a crockpot while still achieving consistently tender and tasty results, using a crockpot may help you save money on food.

Due to the wide variety of options that are now available, it may be challenging to choose the crockpot that will serve you and your family's needs in the best possible manner. Think about how you want to use it, what size it needs, and the features you would like it to have. When shopping for one of these portable appliances, refer to the detailed instructions below for assistance.

2.1 What to Consider When Buying a Crock Pot?

The crockpot is a kind of cooking device that can be found in the majority of homes. Reports estimate that around 83 percent of homes in the US own a slow cooker or a crockpot. Because the food is ready to eat whenever you want to and may be left unattended while you go to work or take your children to sports or other activities, this cooking vessel is convenient for individuals who lead busy lifestyles. Having said that, if you are in the market for a crockpot, you should take your time and make sure that the one you purchase is the one that meets all of your requirements, such as its form, design, dimensions, list of functions, and construction.

Design/Style

There are typically two distinct styles of crockpots on the market: those that have a classic appearance and those that are portable or "travel-friendly" and have lids that can be locked to prevent messy spillage. If you want to transport your slow cooker to events like potluck dinners or social gatherings, choose a portable model rather than a normal one.

Slow cookers come in various designs, dimensions, and surface treatments. If you discover that you need various sizes, a unit with several sized ceramic cuisine bowls in one heating unit, then the Hamilton Beach Model (3 in 1) is the solution. This unit is ideal for those who often prepare meals that need a wide range of temperatures.

Heating Method

The base of most crockpots is designed to tightly contain an insert that can be removed. Sometimes the heating element is just on the bottom, but if you're fortunate, it also goes up the side of the base. Other times, the element is only on the bottom, allowing heat to be more evenly dispersed.

Some crockpots consist of little more than a crock placed on the heating element. This method spreads heat less evenly, and you may need to stir the food more often to keep it from burning. This goes against everything that makes them so appealing to us in the first place.

Lid Material

When using a crockpot, you should avoid opening the lid as often as possible since doing so causes heat to escape and lengthens the cooking process. Crockpots with glass lids allow the user to see what is happening within the appliance without removing the cover and are superior to plastic or models with a more obscure viewing window.

Construction

Although metal crocks are also available, ceramic & porcelain crocks are by far the most common and popular alternatives.

Because they are equally effective at transferring heat, the choice comes down to personal taste. The fact that the crock's lid can be removed makes it much simpler to clean. This is the most significant feature of the crockpot. The ones in which the crock and the heating element are combined into a single unit could be more enjoyable and straightforward to clean.

Timer

Everyone loves it when the crockpot comes equipped with a timer, regardless of whether it is a digital timer or a list of different cooking periods that can be selected. A timer already built into it helps prevent food from being overcooked and mushy, especially if you only sometimes expect to be at home to switch off the crockpot at the appropriate time. There are also delay timers available at the hardware store that you can attach to the crockpot.

Shape

Round and oval are the two most common forms of standard crockpots. Which one is the better option? There needs to be a correct response to this question. Consider what you want to prepare in the crockpot, and let that inform your decision on the design of the appliance. For instance, entire ribs, chicken, or brisket will fit better in an oval form. On the other hand, if you're often preparing beans, soups or stews, the shape doesn't matter as much, and you may purchase the one that fits best in your cupboard or on your counter.

Sear Function

Some crockpots now come with a sear feature that makes it simpler to brown meats, sautés onions, or other vegetables. However, adding this function often increases the crockpot's retail price.

It is possible to design it in two different ways: The first feature allows you to sear food directly in the insert using a setting called "sear" before switching to slow cooking; this might be a helpful feature for those who don't have a cooktop since it allows you to sear food directly in the insert. The second method that searing is possible is if the insert is safe for use on the stovetop:

- Put it on the stovetop.
- Sear the meat directly in the insert.
- Put the seared meat back into the crockpot to complete cooking.

Although the surface area on the bottom of the crockpot's insert may be smaller than that of a frying pan, and you may have to sear the food in batches if you use the first method, the second method allows you to wash one less pan. You may omit this feature if you're trying to save money or plan on doing the fine searing in a pan on the stove.

Accessories

While using a crockpot, you won't need much else; it's a great idea to have some plastic serving cutlery, such as a soup spoon, big

spoon, or slotted spoon, on hand to avoid scratching the ceramic insert. This will keep your crockpot looking its best. Maintaining a crockpot on High for extended periods may cause the bottom of sure models to get rather hot; to prevent damage to your countertop, place a wooden cutting board below the crockpot. Using a slow cooker liner is recommended to speed up the cleaning process. They are compatible with circular or oval crockpots ranging in capacity from about 3 to 6 quarts.

Best Features

For those new to using a crockpot, as well as seasoned veterans, today's appliances provide various functions that simplify the cooking process.

- **Inserts Made of Removable Ceramic:** These inserts, which come included with every device, are extremely simple to clean. Back in the day, crockpots often came with off-white inserts. These days, however, most crockpots feature black inserts. There is a wide variety of colorful designs as well as contemporary stainless steel used for the outside treatments.

- **Programmable Settings:** Most crockpot models are equipped with programmable digital controls, allowing users to schedule the crockpot to operate at a particular time. This function is terrific for those who are required to leave it unattended for some time, for example, during the workplace and who want to return to a dinner that has been prepared and is ready to be served.

- **Automatic Warming Function:** This safety function that activates when your countdown is complete protects you from burning your food and prevents you from wasting it.

- **Different Temperatures:** Although most manual crockpots feature options for warm, high and low temperatures, verifying this information before purchasing is essential. When the dinner is delayed for any reason, the "Keep Warm" option might be beneficial, which is often included as part of the previously stated programmed function. Models that can be programmed often include settings for low and high, and some also function as slow cookers with manual controls.

- **Temperature Probes:** Certain versions of crockpots are equipped with temperature probes that allow you to check the internal temperature of the meat to determine whether it is done cooking. This valuable function prevents you from overcooking or undercooking the meat in your dish.

Cost

A crockpot is helpful in many different situations. The cost is often manageable, and you can expect many years of service out of the equipment. Crockpots may range from ten dollars to one hundred dollars or more for high-end variants due to the variety of functions and capacities available in these appliances.

When a crockpot starts to break down beyond the warranty term, it is often easier to replace the appliance than to pay for a new component or repair it. Because you'll want to use this particular appliance frequently, you'll need to consider the dimensions and capabilities of your purchase.

2.2 How to Choose a Crock Pot?

When you first start shopping for a crockpot device, you can feel like you are being inundated with options since there are so many different models available. Before you dive headfirst into the hunt for the best crockpot for you and your loved ones, the most important thing you can do is organize your thoughts about what you genuinely require, whether it will fit in your cabinet or on the counter, whether it is affordable, and whether or not it will serve its purpose. As you plan, ask yourself some questions.

Usage

You should begin choosing by thinking about how often you will use your crockpot, what kinds of foods you will prepare, and how many people you will be cooking. While shopping, consider whether you want a device with particular capabilities, if you would like the one you can program, and how much money you have in your wallet. How often do you anticipate using the crockpot? Or more often? How much and what kinds of meals are you planning to prepare in it? Will you use it throughout the year or limit its application to the autumn and winter seasons?

Storage

One consideration is the space available in your home for stowing away the item in question when it is not in use. When it comes to storage, smaller kitchens imply less room. When you are not using it to prepare food, a crockpot is something you will probably want to store away in a closet or a pantry.

Capacity

The quickest and most straightforward option is to check the instructions or the box that the equipment arrived in. On the other hand, if you have already thrown it away, you may use a method using water that will work just as well. All that is required of you is to get some water and a regular-sized cup that holds about 8 ounces. Water is measured in cups; 1 quart is equivalent to 4 cups. As a result, you should fill the pot by determining the maximum number of cups of water it can accommodate. For instance, if you can fill your crockpot to the top with about 14 to 16 cups of water, it has a capacity of about 3.5 to 4 quarts.

Food Options

A wide range of food may be prepared successfully in a crockpot, such as beef, chicken, short ribs and something a little out of the ordinary, like soups, lasagna, pasta, mac & cheese and stews.

The further your investigation goes, the more crock pot recipes you'll inevitably come upon. Crockpots may be used to make various traditional foods, for instance. In addition, there are various ideas for producing soups that can be made in a crockpot that you may prepare to warm yourself up when it is chilly outside.

The crockpot will prevent the food from drying out by preserving the food's natural moisture. Be aware that only the portions of the crockpot that can be removed and cooked in the oven are safe, even if the recipe instructs you to do so. As a result, anytime you see low heat specified in the recipe, there is a reasonable probability that you may prepare the meal using your crockpot.

If you have a big crockpot, for example, one with an 8-quart capacity, you could question whether it is necessary to fill it up to its maximum capacity. The good news is that you do not need to purchase an extra crockpot to prepare smaller meals since you can use the one you already have but with a lower capacity. The procedure is as follows.

- To adapt the recipe, have ready a smaller bowl suitable for the oven and fit inside your crockpot. This approach has been put to the test on several occasions, and it has always been successful.

- If you can't locate a bowl of the right size, the dish you're cooking may turn out wrong. The bowl should be filled up to three-quarters of the way, much like a slow cooker when it is being used conventionally.

- Putting too much food in the bowl will take longer for the food to cook since there will need to be more room for the heat to circulate. Some of the components may burn.

- Remember to use a lid on the crockpot, and if at all feasible, try to open it up as little as possible while the food is cooking.

Cooking Time

To choose the correct size of the crockpot, you need to be familiar with the guidelines for slow cooking in a crockpot. First things first, be familiar with your cooking time. The high-temperature option of the crockpot allows sauces to be prepared in the least amount of time, often between one and two hours. Large meat pieces, chicken, roasts and pig shoulders should be cooked on the lowest setting for the maximum time, about 7 hours or more. Cooking times for soups and stews in a crockpot range between 2 to 7 hours.

Keep these basic guidelines in mind at all times:

- Because the crockpot retains moisture, you should only use half of the water or other liquids called for in the recipe except rice. In this crockpot, liquids evaporate more slowly than in a regular pot.

- It is best to wait until the last half an hour of cooking to add the seafood.

- Only fill a crockpot up to its maximum level, regardless of the pot's size you have. Cook it according to the instructions given in the recipe after it is 3/4 full.

- The crockpot is turned on for the last hour to cook the pasta and some soft veggies.

- Rice preparation in a crockpot differs from any other dish, which demands more water than necessary. Additionally, it is distinct from the many methods of rice preparation used by the rice cooker and the instant pot.

- The first step in preparing ground beef is to eliminate the fat by browning and to drain the meat.

- Add dairy items very late, just before serving.

- Cooking fresh ingredients and veggies takes longer than cooking canned or frozen foods.

2.3 How to Choose the Right Size of Crock Pot?

If you want your countertop appliance to be valuable and suitable for your requirements, picking out the right slow cooker is necessary. Various brands offer a decent selection of sizes from one quart up to six or seven quarts. When cooking meat in a crockpot, you should use one quart for every pound of meat you prepare. A chicken weighing 5 pounds might be cooked in a crockpot that has a capacity of about 5 quarts.

1 to 2 Quarts

The most compact crockpots are the most convenient option for individuals or couples who wish to prepare enough food for one meal, for use in a recreational vehicle, or for maintaining the temperature of gravy or dip. These crockpots are considered to be exceptionally tiny. They are sufficient for making dinner for one person and often even for two meals for one person, depending on the cuisine that is being prepared. It is an ideal alternative for someone living alone or sharing a living space with another person. However, you should only expect to be able to cook a part of the dinner in a crockpot that is this little and still have enough food for a refill.

3 to 4 Quarts

These have a capacity twice as large as the previous size but are still very restricted. They work well for intimate lunches or dinners with close friends and family. Again, if you anticipate refills, you will be disappointed since a crockpot of this size can contain enough food to serve up to three or four people.

5 to 6 Quarts

A crock pot of this size should be sufficient for most households. It is a good option for families who do not mind preparing more meals and eating them the next day as leftovers. Because of this, most medium and large families choose this size. They may be used to prepare delicious crockpot recipes to celebrate the arrival of spring or autumn, in addition to a great variety of other foods.

These are an absolute need for households who are always on the go. You may put it to use in dishes like soups, casseroles, and stews. It's not uncommon for households to have a crock pot of this size and use it frequently, in addition to a more compact one used to make sweets or specialized sauces.

7 to 10 Quarts

It is possible to roast significant portions of meat or a whole chicken in this crockpot. It is an excellent option for a family of 6 to 7 people. It can accommodate up to 12 pounds of meat. It is far more extensive than what most families need. That's why it is not commonly used. This quantity is sufficient for a single supper for a big family or for providing a significant amount of leftovers.

Suppose you entertain many people, prefer to create meals ahead of time, produce vast amounts of spaghetti sauce, and so on. In that case, the capacity of your crockpot should also be an essential consideration. The majority of houses are available in more than one size. On the other hand, storage may be an issue for certain people, and if you can only have one size, the 5-quart one is the most flexible option.

2.4 Where to Purchase a Crockpot?

Due to the fact that it is such a popular small home appliance, it can be obtained in a wide variety of locations, such as supermarkets, superstores, home improvement stores, home shops, equipment stores, and even internet merchants. It is entirely up to you whether you purchase it at a physical store or on the internet. It is more convenient for some individuals to examine it in person so they may better understand its dimensions, features, and capabilities. Others like the convenience of having their appliances delivered directly to their front door and the time they save by buying online. In any instance, you should ensure you are familiar with the return policy if there is a problem and the item has to be returned.

Chapter 3: Kitchen Equipment & Crock Pot Tools & Accessories To Have

Do you have a crockpot in your kitchen? It is highly similar to the Instant pot in that it can act as a rice cooker, pressure cooker, slow cooker and so on. Because there are a few critical variances, you must compile your crockpot accessories wish list.

Why is it that as soon as we obtain anything new, the first thing that we want to do is adorn it? This way, you can cook a wider variety of foods and have more fun.

3.1 Crock Pot Tools & Accessories

Even though you don't need all of them to use the crockpot, the fact that you do have them makes things a lot less complicated. Be cautious about verifying the sizes of the crockpot attachments you want to use since only sure of those accessories will be compatible with the crockpot. Since the crockpot express is only offered in a capacity of about six quarts, the larger pans and inserts are incompatible with the device.

Egg Steamer Rack

Thanks to this steamer rack, hard-boiled eggs are one of the first things you can easily make in the crockpot. It is a beautiful opportunity to get acquainted with the device. The eggs turn out beautifully, and it is a breeze to peel them. By using a rack such as this one, it is possible to facilitate the cooking of many eggs at the same time.

Vinyl Decal Stickers

These are unquestionably examples of anything that belongs in the want category rather than the need category. Both Amazon and Etsy have a wide selection of unique styles for customers to choose from. If you have access to a cutting machine, you can produce a vinyl sticker in the blink of an eye.

Springform Bundt Pan

The "pot in pot" method of cooking, used for desserts such as cornbread, cheesecakes, lava cakes, monkey bread and other similar items, requires this bundt pan about seven inches in diameter. You may choose from various recipes if you own anything that can be used for baking.

Gripper Clip

It is a small instrumental piece of equipment. Pull the inner pot out of your crockpot without having your fingers scorched or letting go of the handle. On occasion, many chefs utilize items much like this one, which is incredibly convenient.

Silicone Cooking Rack

One of the most notable distinctions between an Instant pot and a crockpot is the inner pot, which is silicone and may be used as a cooking rack. The inside pot of the crockpot is made of non-stick material, whereas the inner pot of the instant pot is made of stainless steel. For this reason, it is advisable to purchase silicone trivets, pans, and utensils to protect the finish on the inner pot of the crockpot from being damaged.

Parchment Paper Liners

Even though you don't need a liner to cook in the crockpot since the non-stick pan is so simple to clean, consider using one of these liners to prevent aluminum and stainless steel pans from harming the finish on your inner pot.

Springform Pan

You can use it for various pot-in-pot recipes. These are available at most kitchen supply stores. However, it does not have a fluted insert, so you cannot use it to make items like monkey bread or angel food cake.

Mini Loaf Pan

Here is the part where you need to consider the sizes. Because the inner pot is about 8 inches wide, you will only be able to fit something 7 inches in diameter. This is a loaf pan, and although the concept of using it for meatloaf is appealing, you should keep in mind that it is just 6 inches long. In other words, it's a little loaf pan. It is an excellent choice if you prepare food for one or two people.

Silicone Steam Basket

The handles that come with this basket make lifting it much more straightforward. It is large enough to accommodate fish fillets and has high edges preventing water from getting into your cooking.

Mini Springform Pans

It may be used in the same manner as ramekins when preparing smaller individual dishes. Because of their dimensions, they are ideal for preparing handmade "egg muffins" for breakfast.

Silicone Starter Kit

This kit consists of a pot holder, gloves, and a lid. The tiny mitts are ideal for holding the rim of the inner pot and lifting it out. The pot holder will save your counter from scratching, and the closing lid will come in handy when cooking dishes that need more than one pot.

Sealing Rings

These rings are an excellent match for the crockpot. Some scents from cooking are complicated to remove from the silicone gasket; cumin is particularly strong. On the other hand, you can get two more for a relatively low price to change them out while you clean the first set.

Silicone Egg Bites Mold

Even though they aren't the most appetizing to look at, egg bites are an excellent method for including a lot of taste and beneficial components in your morning meal! Imagine them like little omelets, if that helps.

Silicon Baking Cups

If you don't want to spend the money on a mold, you can buy individual baking cups made of silicone and set them inside another dish or on a trivet to cook the food.

Stainless Steel Steam Basket

If you would instead go with steam baskets like this classic one, it would be better as it will fit in the crockpot and cook wonderfully.

Bundt Pan

It has a capacity of about six cups and is ideal for baking bread and more miniature desserts since it is more compact than a standard fluted pan. The measurements of the product are published in a variety of locations. However, the customer evaluations demonstrate that others have had experience utilizing them in their pots.

Disposable Liners

After each meal is prepared in a crockpot, you may quickly and easily clean up the dish with this handy device. What a fantastic way to save time!

Crockpot Rack

This rack may be used in any crockpot that is the standard size, making it ideal for any recipe that calls for a crockpot! It lifts the food above the fat drippings and fluids, which results in improved heat circulation, more uniform baking, and reduced cooking times.

Silicone Spoons

Because the non-stick top of the crockpot gets easily damaged, you must use silicone, wooden, or plastic utensils to stir and scoop food in the crockpot.

Triple-Handled Crock Pot Dipper

This crock pot accessory is the greatest on the market for having guests over. It has a lazy susan feature in addition to its three warmers, each 1 quart in capacity.

Lid Holders

Say farewell to a counter area that is cluttered and disorganized! This incredible appliance, which can be folded up, maintains the lid of your slow cooker at the ideal position, which is just over the rim of the pot.

Silicone Oven Mitts

This tool comes in handy when moving a hot crockpot around the kitchen because of its textured, non-slip grip.

Travel Bag with Insulation

This is the most convenient accessory for your crockpot to take with you wherever. It works well for get-togethers and even celebrations at tailgate events.

Adaptable Cooking Rack

It is a unique and heat-resistant tool that can be bent to fit inside any crockpot, regardless of its dimensions. It will be helpful regardless of the recipe you follow for the crockpot.

Blue Kitchen Utensil Set

You'll discover a collection of the finest tools for use with your crockpot right here. They can withstand high temperatures and are constructed from tough stainless steel, making them suitable for a very long period.

3.2 Kitchen Equipment & Tools For Crock Pot

To ensure that you get the most use out of your crockpot, here are some essential kitchen equipment and tools that should be kept in your kitchen at all times. A crockpot is fantastic all by itself, but when you have a couple of items to the side, it becomes your go-to piece for meal preparation. It is, without a doubt, one of the most incredible appliances that can be found in the kitchen.

Travel Bag

Bringing a crockpot on a trip is the single most annoying thing that can happen, especially if it is not one of the more modern varieties with straps or clips to hold the lid on it. However, there is a way out of this. This bag makes it simple to keep your crockpot clean when traveling to various events, such as fundraising activities, family gatherings, bake sales, etc.

This travel bag is equipped with the following:

- Two handles for carrying it, plus an inside strap to hold it.
- Features include thermal insulation to keep your food warm and zippers to ensure the safety of the slow cooker.

You should consider investing in one of these helpful equipment if you take part in many food-related activities that need you to prepare. It will be a lot less challenging to travel with the food if you do this. In addition, they developed the travel bag out of a simple material to clean if it becomes dirty. With this addition to your crockpot, you really can't go wrong!

Culinary Claws

If shredding meat feels like a lot of work and you don't like doing it, this is the solution to your problem. They feature a soft handle with a broad plastic grip that won't damage your hands and can shred any meat cooked in a crockpot in a matter of minutes without causing discomfort. They do not contain any BPA and can withstand temperatures up to 450 degrees F. In addition, they may be cleaned in a dishwasher, reducing the time spent cleaning.

You are free to put them to use in the following:

- turkey
- beef
- pulled pork
- chicken
- poultry
- roasts

A bonus is that you can use them to toss salads. You must have a pair of these claws to get the most out of your crockpot.

Heat Resistant Grilling Mitts

These oven mitts come in various colors and are made from materials that are safe for the environment. And you won't have to worry about your hands becoming sweaty since they include a soft cotton lining that will wick away any moisture. Because of their texture, which prevents slipping, you won't ever have to worry about losing your hold on your crockpot.

The most significant thing is that they are machine washable, which means that when they get soiled, you can place them in the washing machine to clean them. Does it get any better? Simple to utilize, uncomplicated to clean, and protects your hands well!

Crockpot Liners

After indulging in a delectable dinner prepared in a crockpot, you will be challenged to remove the baked-on filth from the appliance. What is the solution, then? Using a liner in the crockpot makes supper cleanup a breeze. They are compatible with a diverse range of crockpot inserts.

You will no longer need to spend an hour cleaning the baked-on food out of your crockpot after supper. Instead, the only cleanup work that will need to be done is tossing out this stove liner that is free of BPA. Problem fixed. These liners are practical, and the price is more than justified. The kitchen will be spotless, and the cleanup will be a breeze!

Gravy Warmer

The gravy will thicken and become unpleasant if you do not have a suitable location to store it after it is done. This equipment is ideal for maintaining the consistency of the gravy while ensuring that it is kept at the ideal temperature. You will no longer have to wait until the last moment before the holidays to prepare the gravy. Prepare it in advance and keep it ready to eat in this convenient kitchen appliance!

This warmer has a capacity of up to 2 and a half cups of gravy, and since it has a spout, it is effortless to pour the gravy over your meal. In addition, the crock can be cleaned in the dishwasher, which means there will be less mess to clean up after supper.

The best part is that it has a chord that can be removed so that you can carry it straight to the table in the dining room. Your table setting looks even more elegant with this lovely accessory.

Tall Plastic Container

It's different from what you expect! While you are filling the bags with food, use the plastic container as a stand for the bags to keep them upright. This is particularly beneficial when you are freezing liquids with a soupy consistency.

Baggy Rack Stand

This is, without a doubt, the most ingenious device ever created. You've probably experienced the aggravation of placing food in a freezer bag without allowing raw meat to come into contact with the edges or without spilling liquids all over the countertop. This stand is the answer to all of your problems and concerns.

This is an absolute need for using up all those leftovers from the crockpot. This itty-bitty tool will keep the bag open so that you may use both hands to carry the weighty crockpot and put the leftovers away in a hurry without making a huge mess. Just empty your leftovers into the bag you keep in the freezer. After the food has had some time to cool, put the bag down flat in the freezer, and you will have supper ready for the following day.

You can also use these racks to dry your reusable plastic bags, which is a terrific use for them. Wash them well, then hang them inverted over the arms to dry until they are dehydrated. This is a beautiful addition to your kitchen and simplifies preparing meals in a crockpot.

Broiler Rack

This is an excellent method to use when you are cooking meat and do not want the fat to sink into the meat. This rack will gently elevate your food a couple of inches off the bottom of your crockpot so it can cook evenly. Because of this, the heat can circulate more effectively, resulting in shorter cooking times and a more uniform browning over the meat you are preparing. You may use it for fish, chicken, beef, or pig. It's versatile.

Measuring Cups & Spoons

When furnishing a kitchen, one of the first things bought is a set of these. Recipes for the crockpot do not need exact quantities, but a big measuring cup may serve as both a spoon and a measuring cup.

Microwavable Food Containers

One of the most useful accessories for a crockpot is a food container. Why not create an extra large dinner in the crockpot and then keep the leftovers in these convenient containers so that you can take them to work for lunch? You may put them in the freezer and use them to make separate dinners later.

These containers can be heated in the microwave, making them ideal for lunchbox containers or keeping additional portions in the freezer. Instead of eating for lunch, you might bring some nutritious dishes you created at home in your crockpot to bring with you to work. You'll cut down on the calories you consume and the amount of money you spend.

These containers are sturdy, able to be stacked, heated in the microwave, cleaned in the dishwasher, can be frozen, and do not leak. They do not contain any BPA either. If only they would do the cooking for you but wait, you have a crockpot that can do that for you!

Locking Tongs

These tongs measure 12 inches and are available in either stainless steel or silicone.

This help to remove cooked food from the crockpot and brown meats.

Cutting Boards

If you are contemplating whether or not to get a plastic or wooden cutting board, the only thing we can tell you is that we have had both types of cutting boards for years, and the plastic ones are the ones that are used more often since they can be cleaned in the dishwasher.

Crockpot Lid Lock

In addition to coming with a spoon, it has adjustable handles, allowing it to accommodate Crockpots ranging in size from 3 to 8 quarts. It's in the perfect state to take to a potluck! It keeps your dish or gravy safe inside the crockpot and prevents it from spilling or leaking.

Quality Knives

If you are starting, you should invest in at least three high-quality knives. These should include the following:

- Paring knife
- Chef's knife
- Knife with a serrated edge

Heavy Bottomed Pot

If your crockpot does not come with an attachment that allows you to brown meat or sauté veggies, you will need to find another means to do these tasks. You should go for a dutch oven, a pan made of stainless steel, or a cast iron.

Hot Pads

The insert handles on the crockpot become heated to the touch, and the handle on the lid gets hot. Because of this, we need to use a hot pad when we use the crockpot. But certain crockpots do not need hot pads.

Can Opener

Even if you don't use it often, having a can opener on hand is essential when you need one. Many recipes for the crockpot use canned goods such as tomatoes, coconut milk, and other items. Manual can openers are often relatively compact and easy to put away.

Pepper Mill

If you invest in a high-quality model, you may anticipate using the same one for many years.

Mesh Sieve or Colander

The washing of beans or grains, scooping out veggies, and draining pasta are all made easier with the help of these multi-use kitchen utensils.

Spatulas

There are many different spatulas, each with a particular purpose. When using a crockpot,

you first need to get a pair of spatulas made of silicone.

Meat Thermometer

Are you a nervous beginner in the kitchen? You should invest in this instant-read thermometer to guarantee that meats are cooked to the appropriate temperature.

Immersion Blender

Soft vegetables may be puréed straight in the crockpot with this blender to assist in the thickening of soups and sauces.

Vegetable Peeler

Peeling vegetables using a Y-peeler is substantially quicker than peeling vegetables with a paring knife or a swivel peeler.

Citrus Reamer or Juicer

Dishes prepared in a crockpot are given a zingier flavor when the last few minutes of cooking are spent adding a few drops of lemon or lime juice. The usage of a citrus reamer made with wood is straightforward.

Pizza Cutter

To get the most beans cooked in a crockpot, you should consider using them in quesadillas, and using this cutter is the simplest method to cut toasted tortillas. It's possible to cut the flat dumplings needed for chicken and dumplings. And it's likely that every household, whether it has a chef or not, has at least one frozen pizza in the freezer for times of crisis.

Gravy Separator

Fat separators are not often seen as an item that should be considered a "must-have" in the kitchen. On the other hand, if you prepare a lot of fatty meats such as pork shoulder or beef chuck roast, then using this separator may make removing the liquids you want from the pot much more efficient.

Chapter 4: Crockpot Tips & Tricks

A crockpot is a beautiful piece of kitchen equipment that may simplify the preparation of delectable dishes. However, before you go into slow cooking, you need to be sure that you are using your crockpot safely and efficiently. Make use of these suggestions to get the most out of this practical equipment.

4.1 Do's & Don'ts

Make sure you do these:

- Make sure you use a crockpot that is the appropriate size. The crockpot should have between one-half and two-thirds of its capacity total at all times.

- Before putting the meat in the crockpot, brown it first. It is unnecessary to complete this step to ensure food safety, but doing so will enhance the dish's taste and complexity. Once the meat has been placed in the crockpot, it will not brown since crockpots are so good at retaining moisture.

- Make use of the less expensive cuts of beef. Cheaper cuts of meat are often higher in fat or connective tissue than more costly cuts. Since fat and connective tissue both break down during lengthy, wet-heat cooking methods, these techniques will help the meat remain juicy and tender. Lean cuts of meat are often more costly and have a greater propensity to get dry when cooked in a crockpot.

- Add the dairy products towards the end. When exposed to high temperatures, milk, cream, and other dairy products may deteriorate and coagulate. If you wait until the final 15 to 30 minutes to stir these ingredients into the slow cooker, they will have enough time to warm through.

Make sure you don't do these:

- Add a substantial amount of liquid. Keep in mind that meat and vegetables often release a significant amount of liquid when cooking in a crockpot. The cover will prevent this liquid from evaporating. If you add excessive liquid, you may decrease it by cooking on high without the cover for about one to two hours.

- Avoid putting anything that has been frozen straight into the crockpot. Foods that have been frozen may make it take longer for the contents of the slow cooker to reach the acceptable temperature of 140 degrees F and can also increase the risk of becoming sick from foodborne diseases.

- Keep peeking or stirring. The crockpot loses heat whenever the lid is opened, and it takes around twenty to thirty minutes for the appliance to return to the temperature that was previously set. Keep the cover off the pot as little as you can while cooking.

- Never put food that has been cooked in a ceramic crockpot liner into the refrigerator to keep it fresh. Because the ceramic liner is designed to keep heat in, it will prevent the food from cooling down enough when placed in the refrigerator. Before putting food away for storage, you should always move it to a different container.

4.2 Cooking Tips

- Try to load your crockpot with only a little. You should fill it up at most three-quarters of the way as a general guideline. To ensure that the food cooks appropriately, you should aim to fill your slow cooker halfway.

- Always keep the cover on while you're cooking using a crockpot. This will guarantee that the heat is contained inside the cooking area and that the temperature does not drop. If you need to bring food to potlucks and family meals, the lid has clips on both sides to be tightly secured.

- You can cut most recipes in half if you only cook for one or two people. The cooking time may be cut in half. You may increase the amount of food in a crockpot recipe as long as it will still fit in the appliance without filling it more than three-quarters of the way. If the contents of your crockpot are stuffed to the brim, you may need to extend the cooking time.

- It is important to remember not to overcook foods that have a high risk of becoming dry, such as boneless chicken breasts. Check the temperature of the chicken from the inside using a thermometer that provides rapid readings. When the internal temperature of the chicken reaches 165 degrees F at its thickest point, it is ready to eat.

- Pour sauce over the ingredients when making a recipe for chicken stew in a crockpot.

- Unless specifically instructed to do so by the recipe, please do not open your crockpot while it is cooking. When you open the lid of your crockpot, heat is allowed to escape, which causes the total cooking time to increase by about 30 minutes. During the final hour or two of cooking, you may test to see whether the dish is ready by lifting the lid and looking within.

- Another option is adding flavor to veggies by sautéing them in a pan on the stove. After a fast sauté in the oven or on the stove, the taste of certain dishes, notably onions and fresh garlic, is significantly improved.

- A few hardier fresh herbs, like rosemary and thyme, may be added before the food is cooked. However, most fresh herbs should be added after the food has been cooked.

- The cooking time will be reduced when your crockpot is less than filled. To give you an idea, if you want to make shredded chicken in a crockpot, it will take less time to cook two chicken breasts than it takes to prepare six chicken breasts.

- After you have put all of your ingredients into your crockpot, you must never forget to plug it in and turn it on before proceeding with the recipe.

- Before putting everything in the crockpot, brown the ground beef in a skillet. This produces the finest taste and keeps the final product from becoming greasy. Browning adds taste to various types of meat, but it's only sometimes necessary since it may save time.

- It is essential to remove any extra fat from meat before cooking it so that the rendered fat does not go into the sauce. After cooking, you may remove extra fat from the dish by letting it sit for five to ten minutes and then skimming it.

- The addition of fresh citrus and fresh herbs improves the taste of food that has been slow-cooked. It is best to add them after the cooking process to maintain their taste.

4.3 Ingredient Placement Tips

- The rougher pieces of meat and the veggies with the most flavor, such as beef and root vegetables, should go into the crockpot first. In this manner, they will be positioned on the bottom and closer to the heat source. Place more delicate items, like broccoli, higher up on the plate.

- Near the end of the allotted time for cooking, several recipes ask for adding ingredients that need less time to prepare, such as pasta. After the remainder of the cooking is finished, some recipes suggest using the highest heat setting to reduce and thicken a sauce. Even if a recipe calls for a crockpot to be set to high heat for ten minutes to cook pasta or thicken a sauce, the actual amount of time it takes your crockpot to complete these tasks can vary. It will also depend on whether your crockpot was cooking on the high setting when you started it or if it was cooking on the low setting when you started it. Changing the setting from low to high will take more time for the temperature to reach the high setting.

4.4 Meal Prep Tips

- You are not advised to place the items you have prepared in the crockpot insert in the refrigerator once you have done so. Because it could take too long to heat up, cooking in a cold insert raises concerns about the safety of the food being prepared. If the insert is subjected to sudden shifts in temperature, it may break. Many individuals keep prepared foods in the insert of their refrigerator; thus, it is up to you to determine what level of risk you are willing to take and whether or not you feel comfortable doing so.

- You may get a head start on some of the preparation work for a crockpot meal by doing part the night before you intend to use the crockpot. Using this tool, you may mince herbs, carve up meat, and prepare sauces.

- When preparing the ingredients for cooking ahead of time, place them in a bowl, cover them, and keep them in the refrigerator. When you are ready to begin the cooking process, place the meal into the insert of your crockpot.

- Meals from the freezer to the crockpot are a terrific choice for making ahead. Meatballs, taco soup and white chicken chili, are three delectable dishes that can be made in a crockpot using frozen ingredients.

4.5 Other Tips & Tricks

- The high setting on most crockpots is roughly 280 degrees F, while the low setting is approximately 170 degrees F.

- Add fresh herbs at the end of the cooking process to preserve their vibrant tastes.

- By spraying the inside of the crockpot with a non-stick cooking spray before using it, you may avoid cleaning it afterward.

- Put veggies that need to be cooked quickly, such as potatoes, carrots, and other root vegetables, in the bottom of the crockpot, where there will be more moisture, and they will be cooked more quickly.

- The use of liner bags explicitly designed for crockpots makes cleaning simple and fast.

- When it comes to timing, cooking something on a high setting for one hour is equivalent to cooking it on a low setting for two hours.

- Freezing food in sealed and almost complete containers can help prevent freezer burn by minimizing the time the food is exposed to air. After being frozen, items should be consumed three months later.

Chapter 5: Crockpot Cleaning & Maintenance

Carefully maintaining and thoroughly cleaning your crockpot, like any other piece of cookware or device in the kitchen, is essential to achieving the highest possible success with every meal you prepare. Some of us will inevitably experience it. We let something in our crockpot simmer for too long, and as a result, it becomes burned or stuck, leaving us with a mess to clean up. However, alarms are unnecessary since they can be cleaned up with little time and maybe some hard work.

Do you have a mess that is burned on and sticky? Here are some of our most reliable recommendations for keeping your crockpot clean.

5.1 Cleaning Methods & Tips

Always switch off your crockpot, unhook it from the outlet, and give it some time to cool down before beginning the cleaning process. Hot, soapy water or the dishwasher is an acceptable cleaning option for stoneware with a detachable lid made of glass. If you want to clean by hand, make sure to follow these guidelines:

- When washing the stoneware, warm water should be used instead of cold water.

- Scrubbing pads and other abrasive cleaning products are not to be used. Try cleaning using sponges, rags, or a rubber spatula to eliminate particularly tenacious stains.

- Under no circumstances can the heating base ever be submerged in water or any other liquid.

- To get rid of stains and spots, you should clean them using vinegar or a non-abrasive cleaning.

- Stoneware that can be removed may be cleaned either by hand or in the dishwasher.

Baking Soda Method

Every so often, in the same way you've promised yourself you'll finally clear out that cluttered closet, your crockpot also needs a thorough cleaning. This comprehensive and in-depth deep clean recipe is ideal for spring cleaning, which is the best time of year to make your crockpot appear as good as new.

So put on your rubber gloves, gather your cleaning tools, and work on this formula as soon as possible.

- Fill your crockpot with water until it reaches the line that indicates where you should stop adding food.

- Add a half cup of distilled white vinegar to a crockpot with 3 quarts and a full cup to a crockpot with 6 quarts.

- Slowly pour a half cup of baking soda into a crockpot with 3 quarts or a full cup with 6 quarts. Wait for the bubbles to subside before adding just a tiny bit more.

- Cover and simmer on the low setting in your crockpot for one hour with the lid on.

- When the timer goes off, take the lid off the container and begin cleaning with a gentle sponge and as much force as is necessary.

- After that, you should wait until the crockpot has cooled down before washing it in the sink using warm soapy water.

- Place it on the counter where it can air dry.

Basic Method

The stoneware crock component of your crockpot may be cleaned following these instructions. Keep water up to the bottom of your crockpot, the portion you plug in. Apply some home cleanser using a cloth or sponge that has been dampened, and then wipe the area clean.

You should always begin with the approaches that are the least difficult and the most natural initially, and then, if the section that was burned on is still there, you should continue to the next level.

Hot Soapy Water

To clean a crockpot disaster, soaking it in hot, soapy water works for around 99 percent of the time. Put the crockpot in the sink, add some dish soap, and then fill it with the hottest water from the faucet that you can manage. Wash it as you usually would after letting it soak for an hour to two.

Dishwasher

If your crockpot is suitable for the dishwasher and the debris inside is just slightly stuck, you may place it in the dishwasher to clean it. The detergents used in contemporary automatic dishwashers are formulated to cut through oil and food adhered to surfaces.

Oven Cleaners

Oven cleaner should only be used as a last resort. Oven cleaning is hazardous. It is unpleasant to breathe in the vapors, and the substance itself is rather revolting. However, if all else fails, you may try drying out your crockpot as well as you can with a paper towel or another item, spraying oven cleaning on the charred remains and letting it set for several hours or even overnight. If you have burned things stuck on your crockpot, you may need to keep applying the item, waiting, rinsing, and scrubbing until you get it all off.

5.2 Maintenance Tips

Your crockpot has probably supplied you with many smiles and laughs over the years, and it is only fitting that you treat it with the highest level of respect possible. And regardless of how often you give your stoneware, detachable lid, or even the crockpot itself a thorough cleaning, with time, all of these components will get worn down due to natural occurrences.

Have a desire for a pot roast? Is a hearty stew on the menu for your family tonight? In any case, the preparation of these meals will need some time. Slow cooking in a crockpot is an excellent method to prepare flavorful meals without being confined to the kitchen. Even though you probably don't consider it much before turning on your crockpot, cooking machines like that can be harmful if they aren't appropriately utilized. Even though it doesn't happen often, your crockpot might start a fire. Check out these helpful suggestions before you throw that brisket into your crockpot.

- Place your crockpot in the center of a table or counter and keep it far away from the edge of the surface. Also, make an effort to conceal the cable. It just takes a hyperactive pet or an inquisitive child to knock over the slow cooker, which will then spill all of its hot contents over the floor.

- Crockpots come in many sizes, from a modest 1.5 quarts to a vast 8 quarts. Check the directions provided by the manufacturer twice before you begin filling it. Most recipes call for filling a crockpot between one-half and two-thirds of the way complete. The contents can boil over if you overfill it, but if you don't add enough liquid, your supper might be burned.

- Putting your crockpot in a position where it is too near to a wall is asking for trouble. Be safe; give yourself a margin of at least 6 inches around your crockpot.

- If you want to cook while away from home, consider investing in a crockpot that can be programmed. After a certain amount of time, these models will automatically transition to a lower temperature. This function helps prevent food from being burned and residences from catching fire.

- Electrical equipment should never be used near water. When you are using your crockpot, be sure to keep it out of the kitchen sink and any other sources of water. Also, avoid touching the plug with damp hands at any time.

- On the counter in the kitchen is where you should put the slow cooker for the greatest results. Nevertheless, any heat-resistant and flat surface would do in a pinch. It is best to keep your crockpot on a smooth surface, and you should never put it anywhere near materials that might quickly get entangled, such as towels, curtains, or napkins.

- Cooking is done at a more leisurely pace using a crockpot. Keep the heat low in your crockpot, particularly if you want to cook anything overnight. The correct temperature is the foundation of safe crockpot use.

- It's a fantastic way to save time to use a crockpot for cooking meals overnight, but is it safe to keep a crockpot on while you sleep with the food still inside? Absolutely! If you are okay with turning your crockpot on while you're out at work, you should be okay with keeping it on while you sleep.

- The ability to prepare meals in a crockpot without standing over a hot stovetop has contributed to the appliance's widespread adoption. But is it risky to keep a crockpot running for the whole day? Yes! Because of the relatively lower temperature at which crockpots cook, it is common practice to leave the device on for anywhere between four and eight hours.

- What can you do while the food slowly cooks all day? You can go to work, errands, get chores done, or relax. There is no cause for alarm provided that the directions provided by the manufacturer use the crockpot and that it was not a hand-me-down from your great-grandmother. Make sure it's on a level area and away from any walls when you put it there.

- On the other hand, if your crockpot is rather old, consider replacing it. While retro kitchenware from the 1970s has a great retro aesthetic, you shouldn't use it for food preparation. Make sure your crockpot is up to date with the latest safety regulations before leaving it on all night. For instance, it should be considered dated if it has a cloth cord. Get rid of your crockpot immediately if it has an insert linked to it. Consider purchasing a new model if the unit no longer warms up effectively.

- Crockpot liners are your last option for minimizing cleanup while using your crockpot. These liners are handy for making cleaning a breeze; all you need to do is throw away the trash. After each usage, give your crockpot a quick wipe-down with a damp cloth to ensure it stays in the best condition possible.

Chapter 6: Frequently Asked Questions

Do you have questions regarding how to prepare food using a crockpot? Do you need help deciding which crockpot to purchase? Find the answers you're looking for in this chapter.

What sets a slow cooker different from a crock pot?

There is no distinction between the two. The name brand "Crock-Pot" has become synonymous with the word "slow cooker," a generic term. The parent business of the rival is the owner of the registered trademark for the Crock-Pot brand of slow cookers. And the generic name for all other brands is simply a slow cooker.

Is the bottom coating of the crockpot toxic?

It is disturbing to think that harmful elements may leak into food, but the good news is that lead-free glazes are mandated to be used by most ceramic manufacturers nowadays. This means that new, intact, good-quality ceramic crockpots are a relatively safe choice.

Is cooking in a crockpot risky?

It is risk-free to prepare food in a crockpot. They can achieve a temperature of 209 degrees Fahrenheit, which, when combined with the fact that food is prepared in a wet environment for an extended length of time, ensures that common germs such as E. coli, salmonella, and botulism are safely destroyed. Be careful to adhere to the cooking periods specified in the recipe you are using to ensure that your food, particularly your meat, is cooked appropriately.

What do I do if the coating on the bottom gets scratched?

Don't care much about the minor scratches. Try cleaning the bigger ones by using the methods mentioned in chapter 5. Before cleaning your crockpot, you should always turn it off, disconnect it from the electrical outlet, and let it cool down first. Either the dishwasher or some hot soapy water may be used to clean the lid of the container. Regarding models that include stoneware that can be removed, you may take the stoneware out and either put it in the dishwasher or wash it by hand with hot soapy water. Scrubbing pads and harsh cleaning solutions are not permitted to be used. In most cases, removing any residue may be done using a cloth, sponge, or rubber spatula. Vinegar or a non-abrasive cleanser may remove watermarks and other stains off surfaces.

The stoneware and the lid cannot survive quick fluctuations in temperature, just like any other excellent pottery. When washing the stoneware, warm water should be used instead of cold water. The outside of the heating base may be cleaned using a gentle cloth and water that has been soap-treated. Dry with a rag. You should not clean with abrasive products. Under no circumstances can the heating base be submerged in water or other liquid.

How can I prevent the food from drying out?

Unless it is essential, refrain from lifting the cover while the food is cooking. This not only lengthens the cooking time but also allows valuable moisture to be lost. In addition, check to see that you have included enough liquid in the crockpot so that the food stays moist. It doesn't have to be much, but even a tiny amount will help your food steam a little bit, which will assist keep some of the moisture in the dish.

Also, ensure that your recipes call for an appropriate cooking time so the food will be well-spent when you arrive home. For instance, a meal that asks for 8 hours of cooking time should be acceptable on low for up to 10 hours, while a recipe that only calls for 5 to 6 hours of cooking time could be overdone if you don't arrive home for 10 hours after it calls for it to be cooked.

What to do if the "release valve: doesn't hold steam?

It must be pressed in before it will fit. Steam will only escape the steam release valve if firmly lodged in its position. What is this, exactly? The solution to this problem is to depress the valve and then repeatedly move it from the wealing position to the venting position and back again so it sits correctly.

Is it necessary to stir the food during cooking in the crockpot?

Because of how a crockpot works, it is unnecessary to stir the food throughout the cooking process unless the recipe specifies that you should do so. Taking the lid off a crockpot to stir the food causes the appliance to lose a substantial amount of heat, making the cooking process take much longer.

Is it better to buy a model with a ceramic bottom or stainless steel insert?

When it comes to crockpots, the cooking pot may be manufactured out of a variety of different materials, depending on the kind of crockpot. Ceramics and aluminum are the most often seen. Each kind of material has a unique combination of advantages and disadvantages.

Because they are non-reactive, ceramic crockpots will not impart any potentially hazardous chemicals or poisons into the food cooked in them. They are also incredibly sturdy, ensuring they will survive very long. On the other hand, compared to aluminum crockpots, they often have a higher price tag and are more cumbersome.

Aluminum crockpots are not only far less expensive than ceramic ones, but they are also significantly easier to handle. However, if they come into contact with certain meals, they may cause those foods to develop a metallic flavor.

Which slow cooker is best to buy?

These are the best to buy:

- Crock-Pot Cook & Carry Slow Cooker, Programmable, 6-Quart

- Hamilton Beach Defrost Slow Cooker, 6-Quart

- All-Clad Gourmet Plus Slow Cooker with All-in-One, 7-Quart

- Crock-Pot Oval Manual Slow Cooker, 7-Quart

Why does cooking with a ceramic pot without liquid create cracks?

If a crockpot is malfunctioning or improperly handled, the ceramic insert or the glass crock will break. Extreme temperature shifts, placing it on fire on your cooktop, or laying it down too firmly on a flat, solid surface are all common causes of cracking.

What capacity should I look for in a crockpot?

This will partly rely on the number of people you are cooking for and the kind of food you are doing.

- One to one and a half quarts is the perfect serving size for singles.

- For a pair, a 2 1/2- 3 1/2 pint is excellent.

- Choose a container between 3.5 and 4.5 quarts if you have between three and four people in your home.

- Choose a unit with 5 quarts of capacity if you have a family of five.

- The greatest choice for serving food to six or more people is a 6-quart pot.

What can I do if the gasket becomes impregnated with odors?

To rid an object made of silicone of unpleasant odors, one of the most typical advice is to let it soak for some time in a solution consisting of equal parts water and white vinegar.

What to do if steam keeps coming out of the crockpot?

Most crockpots include holes in the top that allow the steam to exit naturally. Therefore, a crockpot should allow a tiny amount of steam to escape. If you discover that your crockpot is letting out a significant amount of steam, this may cause your cooking times to be affected, and you may need to change the lid.

The steam release valve will not be secured in the correct position. While cleaning the lid, if you remove the steam release valve, you may need help putting it back in the right place. It must be pressed in before it will fit. Steam will only escape from the valve if it is firmly lodged in its position.

Can a crockpot go in the fridge?

Because the electrical components and wiring in crockpots are vulnerable to damage when exposed to water and cold, it is not a good idea to store the appliance in the refrigerator. Even though the ceramic dish that rests in the base can be removed so that it may be cleaned, it can also be used to store food in the refrigerator.

Are the slow cooker liners safe?

Liners for slow cookers can withstand temperatures of up to 400 degrees F, making them suitable for use on the device's low, medium, and high settings. Choose liners that are made of nylon, heat-resistant, and BPA-free. These liners can withstand the stress of robust ingredients without ripping.

Can a crockpot go in the dishwasher?

Before cleaning your crockpot, you must ensure that it is turned off, unplugged from the electrical outlet, and allowed to cool. Either the dishwasher or some hot soapy water may be used to clean the lid of the container. Regarding models that include stoneware that can be removed, you may take the stoneware out and either put it in the dishwasher or wash it by hand with hot soapy water.

Chapter 7: 1 Week Meal Plan

To get the most out of your crockpot experience, stick to this meal plan for the next 7 days. It includes a daily meal plan, including breakfast, lunch, and dinner, all based on the recipes in this cookbook. This diet is based on 2,000 calories per day. It is usually recommended that you drink a sufficient amount of water, even if water is only sometimes included as a component of each meal. Simply dividing your whole-body weight in half and drinking that many ounces of water daily will give you an accurate estimate of the amount of water your body needs daily.

Here's a sample of a one-week meal plan, depending on 2,000 kcal each day:

Day 1

- **Breakfast:** Breakfast Casserole
- **Lunch:** Pineapple Chicken Rice Bowl
- **Dinner:** Tuscan Chicken

Day 2

- **Breakfast:** Mexican Tater Tot Casserole
- **Lunch:** Fish Pie
- **Dinner:** Sticky Chicken With Noodles

Day 3

- **Breakfast:** Breakfast Quinoa
- **Lunch:** Butternut Curry & Noodles
- **Dinner:** Thai Pork Curry

Day 4

- **Breakfast:** Carrot Cake Oatmeal
- **Lunch:** Chicken Fajita Soup
- **Dinner:** Honey Bourbon Chicken

Day 5

- **Breakfast:** Multi-Grain Hot Cereal
- **Lunch:** Barley, Shrimp & Corn Salad
- **Dinner:** Beef Pot Roast

Day 6

- **Breakfast:** Hashbrown Sausage Casserole
- **Lunch:** Kidney Beans Curry
- **Dinner:** Cajun Chicken Alfredo

Day 7

- **Breakfast:** Cauliflower Hashbrowns
- **Lunch:** Pinto Beans
- **Dinner:** Balsamic Pork Tenderloin

Chapter 8: Breakfast Recipes

1. Breakfast Casserole

Prep Time: 10 minutes

Cook Time: 3 hours

Servings: 2

Ingredients

- 1 tsp of salt
- ½ tsp of pepper
- ¼ tsp of garlic powder
- ¼ tsp of dry mustard
- ¼ cup of onions
- ½ cup of milk
- 1 ½ cups of cheddar cheese
- 1 cup of bacon
- 4 eggs
- 1 cup of hash brown potatoes

Instructions

- Blend the eggs with all ingredients, except milk, in a bowl.
- Add milk and whisk well.
- Place potatoes in a single layer, along with onions and some bacon, in a crockpot.
- Season with pepper and shredded cheese on top. Make two to three layers.
- Cook for 3-4 hours on low until eggs are done.

Nutrients: Kcal: 216, Fats: 12 g, Total Carbs: 26 g, Proteins: 19 g.

2. Mexican Tater Tot Casserole

Prep Time: 10 minutes

Cook Time: 2 hours

Servings: 2

Ingredients

- 15 oz of ground beef
- 2 cloves of garlic, minced
- 16 oz of tater tots frozen
- 6 oz of Velveeta Cheese, cubed
- ½ cup of taco spice
- ½ cup of shredded cheese

Instructions

- Sauté beef with garlic until browned.
- Add a single layer of tater tots with ground beef, all seasonings and Velveeta on top in a crockpot.
- Cook for 2 hours on low.
- Before serving, add cheese and let it melt for 10 minutes.

Nutrients: Kcal: 308, Fats: 27 g, Total Carbs: 53 g, Proteins: 27 g.

3. Crockpot Steel Cut Oats with Banana

Prep Time: 10 minutes

Cook Time: 4 hours

Servings: 2-4

Ingredients

- ½ tsp of kosher salt
- ½ tsp of nutmeg
- 1 ½ tsp of ground cinnamon
- 4 cups of water
- 2 tsp of pure vanilla extract

- 2 cups of milk
- 3 tbsp of ground flaxseed
- 2 mashed, ripe bananas
- 1 ½ cups of steel-cut oats

Instructions

- Add all the ingredients to a crockpot. Stir continuously to combine it well.
- Let it cover and cook on low for 2-4 hours until the oats are soft.
- Top with desired toppings and serve.

Nutrients: Kcal: 219, Fats: 5 g, Total Carbs: 28 g, Proteins: 7 g.

4. Crockpot Hash Brown Casserole

Prep Time: 10 minutes

Cook Time: 1 hour 30 minutes

Servings: 2

Ingredients

- ½ tsp of onion powder
- ½ tsp of garlic powder
- ¼ tsp of dried thyme
- 1 tsp of dried parsley
- 1 tsp of chicken bouillon powder
- 1 cup of milk
- 1/3 cup of all-purpose flour
- 1 tsp of Dijon mustard
- ½ cup of sour cream
- 1 cup of chicken broth
- ¼ cup of finely diced mushrooms
- ½ cup of diced yellow onion
- 1 ½ clove of garlic, minced
- 1 ½ cups of shredded Cheddar cheese
- 10 oz of hash browns, shredded
- 3 tbsp of unsalted butter

Instructions

- Melt the butter in a skillet, add diced onion and mushrooms, and sauté for 5-7 minutes.
- Add remaining seasonings to the skillet and sauté for 1 minute.
- Ladle chicken broth along with flour and whisk well. Gradually add milk and cook until thickened. Simmer and add Dijon mustard and sour cream.
- Ladle this to the crockpot and add hash browns with cheddar cheese.
- Mix it well and put a few sheets of paper towel between the lid and the crockpot. Cook on high for 2-3 hours.

Nutrients: Kcal: 347, Fats: 34 g, Total Carbs: 48 g, Proteins: 26 g.

5. Breakfast Quinoa

Prep Time: 10 minutes

Cook Time: 4 hours

Servings: 2

Ingredients

- ¼ tsp of salt
- 2 cups of water
- 2 tbsp of maple syrup or raw honey
- 1 cup of canned coconut milk
- 1 cup of uncooked quinoa

Instructions

- Put rinsed quinoa with all ingredients in a crockpot and cover it with a lid.
- Cook on low flame for 4 hours. Serve hot with milk.

Nutrients: Kcal: 126, Fats: 17 g, Total Carbs: 29 g, Proteins: 7 g.

6. Crockpot Potatoes

Prep Time: 10 minutes

Cook Time: 2 hours 15 minutes

Servings: 2

Ingredients

- 1 tsp of kosher salt
- 1 tsp of pepper
- 2 tsp of seasoned salt
- 2 tsp of smoked paprika
- 3 cloves of garlic minced
- 2 tbsp of unsalted butter diced
- 2 tbsp of extra-virgin olive oil
- ½ medium onion
- 1 red bell pepper
- 1 green bell pepper
- 5 oz of potatoes

Instructions

- Spray the crockpot with oil. Add all the ingredients to the pot with butter.
- Spoon olive oil on the top, cover and cook for 2 hours.
- Stir and cook until potatoes become tender.

Nutrients: Kcal: 192, Fats: 6 g, Total Carbs: 32 g, Proteins: 4 g.

7. French Toast Casserole

Prep Time: 30 minutes

Cook Time: 2 hours 30 minutes

Servings: 2

Ingredients

- 1 cup of milk
- 1/2 tsp of salt
- ½ cup of brown sugar
- ¼ tsp of ground nutmeg
- 1 ½ tsp of cinnamon
- 1 tsp of vanilla extract
- ¼ cup of maple syrup
- 2 tbsp of salted butter sliced
- 2 oz of sandwich bread
- ½ cup of chopped pecans
- 4 large eggs

Instructions

- Spray the crockpot with oil and layer pecans on the bottom.
- In another bowl, beat the eggs with milk and other ingredients.
- Spoon the egg mixture over the bread and pecans in the crockpot and mix well.
- Cover the crockpot and cook for 2 hours on high.

Nutrients: Kcal: 371, Fats: 17 g, Total Carbs: 44 g, Proteins: 11 g.

8. Carrot Cake Oatmeal

Prep Time: 10 minutes

Cook Time: 3 hours

Servings: 2

Ingredients

- ½ cup of golden raisins
- ½ tsp of ground nutmeg
- 1 tsp of ground cinnamon
- 2 cups of almond milk
- 2 cups of coconut milk
- 1 cup of steel-cut oats
- 1 cup of finely grated carrot

Instructions

- Grease the bottom of the crockpot.
- Fill the pot with steel-cut oats.
- Combine all ingredients with oats.

- Cook on low for 2-3 hours.
- Sprinkle brown sugar, coconut flakes, and chopped pecans on top before serving.

Nutrients: Kcal: 184, Fats: 4 g, Total Carbs: 34 g, Proteins: 5 g.

9. Mocha Coffee

Prep Time: 10 minutes

Cook Time: 2 hours

Servings: 2

Ingredients

- ¾ cup of coconut sugar
- 1 tsp of vanilla extract
- 1 ¾ cups of almond milk
- ⅓ cup of unsweetened cocoa powder
- 1 ½ cups of strong brewed coffee

Instructions

- In a container, combine all the ingredients and spoon them into the crockpot.
- Cook for 2 hours on low.
- Spoon the milk into the cups and serve hot.

Nutrients: Kcal: 137, Fats: 2 g, Total Carbs: 30 g, Proteins: 2 g.

10. Pumpkin Pie Oatmeal

Prep Time: 10 minutes

Cook Time: 3 hours

Servings: 2

Ingredients

- 2 ½ cups of water
- ¼ tsp of salt
- 1 tsp of pumpkin pie spice
- ½ tsp of cinnamon
- 1 tsp of vanilla

- 3 tbsp of maple syrup
- 1 cup of pumpkin puree
- 1 ½ cups of unsweetened almond milk
- 1 cup of steel-cut oats

Instructions

- Grease the crockpot with butter.
- Add all the ingredients into the pot and mix well.
- Cover and cook for 2-3 hours. Set the oats aside and let them set at room temperature.
- Top the oats bowl with pecans, maple syrup and almond milk.

Nutrients: Kcal: 242, Fats: 4 g, Total Carbs: 45 g, Proteins: 8 g.

11. Giant Blueberry Pancake

Prep Time: 10 minutes

Cook Time: 55 minutes

Servings: 2

Ingredients

- 2 tbsp of white sugar
- 2 ½ tsp of baking powder
- 2 cups of all-purpose flour
- 1 tsp of vanilla
- 1 ½ cups of milk
- ¼ cup of fresh blueberries
- 2 large eggs

Instructions

- In a container, beat the eggs with milk and vanilla until blended well.
- In another container, mix dry ingredients.
- Add the egg mixture to the flour and make the batter.
- Spoon the batter into the crockpot and top with blueberries.

- Cook for 1 hour and check with the help of a spatula when the pancakes are done.

Nutrients: Kcal: 174, Fats: 2 g, Total Carbs: 30 g, Proteins: 6 g.

12. Apple Crisp

Prep Time: 15 minutes

Cook Time: 3 hours

Servings: 2

Ingredients

- 1/4 tsp of salt
- ½ cup of sugar
- ½ cup of brown sugar
- 1 tsp of cinnamon
- ¼ tsp of nutmeg
- 1 tbsp of cornstarch
- 1 tbsp of lemon juice
- 1 cup of walnuts chopped
- 1/2 cup of cold butter
- 1 cup of all-purpose flour
- 3 cups of apples peeled and sliced

Instructions

- Mix flour, brown sugar, cinnamon, sugar, nutmeg, and salt in a bowl.
- Grate the butter and add walnuts. Toss well.
- Grease the crock pot with oil and place the apple slices in the center of the crockpot.
- Combine the remaining ingredients in a bowl
- Cook on high for 2 hours. Serve with desired toppings.

Nutrients: Kcal: 97, Fats: 14 g, Total Carbs: 18 g, Proteins: 16 g.

13. Tea Latte

Prep Time: 15 minutes

Cook Time: 3 hours

Servings: 2-3

Ingredients

- 4-star anise
- 1 tsp of whole allspice
- 4 cinnamon sticks
- 1 tsp of whole cloves
- 1/3 cup of honey
- 4 cups of whole milk
- 3 cups of boiling water
- 2 tbsp of chai tea leaves

Instructions

- Cook the tea leaves in the crockpot with boiling water for 15 minutes on high.
- Add all the ingredients to the pot.
- Mix, cover, and cook for 2 ½ to 3 hours on high.
- Strain and serve with whipped cream and cinnamon.

Nutrients: Kcal: 251, Fats: 5 g, Total Carbs: 39 g, Proteins: 8 g.

14. Peach Crisp

Prep Time: 15 minutes

Cook Time: 3 hours

Servings: 2

Ingredients

- 1 tbsp of lemon juice
- 1/4 tsp of salt
- 3 tbsp of brown sugar
- ¼ tsp of allspice
- ¼ tsp of baking soda
- 1 tsp of baking powder

- 1/2 tsp of ground cinnamon
- ¾ cup of all-purpose flour
- 4 tbsp of unsalted butter
- 1 tsp of pure vanilla extract
- 1 cup of rolled oats
- 5 peaches

Instructions

- Grease the crockpot with butter.
- In a bowl, combine peach slices with vanilla, lemon juice and brown sugar.
- Layer the peach mixture on the bottom of the crockpot.
- In another bowl, combine all remaining ingredients with the butter.
- Cook on high for 3 hours until it becomes crisp.

Nutrients: Kcal: 67, Fats: 9 g, Total Carbs: 18 g, Proteins: 4 g.

15. Banana Bread

Prep Time: 5 minutes

Cook Time: 2 hours

Servings: 2

Ingredients

- ½ tsp of salt
- ½ cup of sugar
- ½ tsp of baking soda
- 1 tsp of baking powder
- ½ cup of chopped walnuts
- 1 ½ cups of all-purpose flour
- 1/3 cup of softened butter
- 1 cup of ripe bananas mashed
- 2 eggs beaten

Instructions

- Mix butter with sugar and eggs into the bowl and mix well.
- Combine all dry ingredients in a separate bowl.
- Add bananas to the sugar mixture and mix. Drizzle some chopped walnuts and stir.
- Grease the crockpot and spoon the batter in it.
- Cook on high for 2-3 hours until it's done.

Nutrients: Kcal: 147, Fats: 14 g, Total Carbs: 12 g, Proteins: 6 g.

16. Granola

Prep Time: 15 minutes

Cook Time: 3 hours

Servings: 2

Ingredients

- ¼ tsp of salt
- ½ cup of honey
- 2 cups of shredded coconut
- 2 cups of chopped nuts
- 1 cup of dried fruit
- 4 cups of oats
- ½ cup of coconut oil, melted

Instructions

- Spray the crockpot with oil. Add all ingredients and mix.
- Let the coconut oil melt and add honey. Spoon the mixture into the pot and cover evenly.
- Stir everything and cook on low for 2-2 ½ hours.
- Store in an air-tight container when done.

Nutrients: Kcal: 260, Fats: 5 g, Total Carbs: 28 g, Proteins: 7.6 g.

17. Multi-Grain Hot Cereal

Prep Time: 5 minutes

Cook Time: 4 hours

Servings: 2

Ingredients

- 1 tsp of cinnamon
- 2 tsp of vanilla extract
- ½ cup of water
- 2 apples
- 1 cup of wheat berries
- 1 cup of brown rice
- 1 cup of oats, steel-cut
- 1 cup of quinoa

Instructions

- Add all the ingredients to a greased crockpot—cover, and cook on low for 4 hours.
- Sprinkle dried fruits or raisins before serving.

Nutrients: Kcal: 65, Fats: 1 g, Total Carbs: 4 g, Proteins: 4 g.

18. Mexican Casserole

Prep Time: 15 minutes

Cook Time: 2 hours 30 minutes

Servings: 2

Ingredients

- 2 tbsp of cilantro
- 1 cup of taco seasoning
- 1 cup of milk
- 1 tbsp of green onion
- 1 medium onion diced
- ½ green bell pepper diced
- ½ red bell pepper diced
- large eggs

- ¾ cup of ground sausage
- 1 cup of cheddar cheese shredded
- 2 cups of frozen hash brown potatoes

Instructions

- Fry sausages with onions in a pan. Mix eggs with milk, cheese and seasoning mix.
- Grease the crockpot with oil. Add hashbrowns, sausage, and red and green pepper in layers—spread cilantro over it.
- Spoon egg mixture into the pot, cover and cook for 2 ½ hours until eggs are done.

Nutrients: Kcal: 405, Fats: 27 g, Total Carbs: 17 g, Proteins: 20 g.

19. Veggie Omelets

Prep Time: 10 minutes

Cook Time: 2 hours

Servings: 2

Ingredients

- ½ tsp of chili powder
- ½ tsp of ground pepper
- 1/2 tbsp of dried Italian Seasoning
- ¼ cup of milk
- 2 cloves of garlic, minced
- ½ tsp of salt
- 1 small yellow onion, finely chopped
- ½ tsp of garlic powder
- 1 small red bell pepper, diced
- 1 cup of broccoli florets
- 1 cup of shredded cheddar cheese
- 1/4 cup of grated parmesan cheese
- 4 large eggs

Instructions

- Grease the crockpot with butter. Beat the eggs with salt, milk, black pepper, parmesan, garlic powder, Italian seasoning, and chili powder in a bowl.
- Put all the veggies in the crockpot. Stir the egg mixture over it.
- Cook on high for 2 hours until eggs are cooked properly.
- Add cheese on top and let it melt.

Nutrients: Kcal: 166, Fats: 11 g, Total Carbs: 5 g, Proteins: 12 g.

20. Caramel Pecan Sticky Buns

Prep Time: 15 minutes

Cook Time: 3 hours

Servings: 2

Ingredients

- tbsp of melted butter
- ¾ cup of brown sugar
- 1 tsp of ground cinnamon
- ¼ cup of chopped pecans
- 5 oz of tubes of biscuits

Instructions

- Spray the crockpot with butter.
- Combine brown sugar, cinnamon, and chopped nuts in a bowl.
- Add the biscuits to the sugar mixture and layer the biscuits in the crockpot.
- Cover and cook on high for 1 ½ to 2 hours.

Nutrients: Kcal: 227, Fats: 11 g, Total Carbs: 29 g, Proteins: 3 g.

21. Fried Apples

Prep Time: 10 minutes

Cook Time: 2 hours

Servings: 2

Ingredients

- ¼ cup of sugar
- ¼ cup of brown sugar
- 1 tsp of ground cinnamon
- 2 tbsp of cornstarch
- 2 tsp of lemon juice
- 1 tsp of vanilla extract
- ¼ cup of salted butter
- 5 oz of crisp honey apples

Instructions

- Add apples and all remaining ingredients to the crockpot.
- Toss evenly until the apples are coated.
- Cook for 2 hours on high until the apples are crisped.

Nutrients: Kcal: 319, Fats: 10 g, Total Carbs: 62 g, Proteins: 1 g.

22. Yeast Bread

Prep Time: 15 minutes

Cook Time: 2 hours

Servings: 2

Ingredients

- 1 ½ tsp of salt
- 2 ¼ tsp of instant yeast
- 3 ½ cups of bread flour
- 1 ½ cups of warm water

Instructions

- Put the yeast and salt with some warm water in the flour bowl to make the dough.
- Whisk well and add water as desired.

Roll the dough in a ball, cover it with a plastic sheet, and set it at room temperature for 6-8 hours.

- Place the parchment paper in the crockpot.
- Flatten the dough on a board and make little balls of it. Put these balls in the crockpot.
- Cover with a double-lining towel and cook for 2 hours.
- Remove the parchment and place the bread on a plate. Slice the bread before serving.

Nutrients: Kcal: 159, Fats: 0 g, Total Carbs: 33 g, Proteins: 5 g.

23. Breakfast Grits

Prep Time: 5 minutes

Cook Time: 4 hours

Servings: 2

Ingredients

- 4 tbsp of butter
- 2 tsp of salt
- 2 cups of cream
- cups of water
- 12 oz of grated cheddar cheese
- 1 ½ cups of stone ground grits

Instructions

- Grease the crockpot with butter. Add grits with water and salt.
- Cook on low for 4 hours.
- Add cream, butter, and grated cheese before serving.

Nutrients: Kcal: 357, Fats: 28 g, Total Carbs: 17 g, Proteins: 10 g.

24. Berry Compote

Prep Time: 5 minutes

Cook Time: 1 hour

Servings: 2

Ingredients

- ½ cup of granulated sugar
- 2 tbsp of water
- 1 tbsp of orange juice
- 1 tbsp of orange zest
- 2 tbsp of cornstarch
- 3 cups of frozen mixed berries

Instructions

- Add all ingredients in a greased crockpot, except corn starch water.
- Cook for 1 hour on low.
- In a bowl, combine cornstarch and water.
- Pour cornstarch water into the berry mixture and combine.
- Cover and cook for another 10-15 minutes until thickened.

Nutrients: Kcal: 89, Fats: 11 g, Total Carbs: 18 g, Proteins: 6 g.

25. Blueberry French Toast

Prep Time: 10 minutes

Cook Time: 4 hours

Servings: 2

Ingredients

- 1 tsp of salt
- 1 cup of brown sugar
- 1 tsp of cinnamon
- 1 tsp of maple syrup
- 1 tsp of vanilla
- 1 ½ cups of milk
- ¼ cup of melted butter

- 1 ½ cups of blueberries, frozen
- 4 slices of bread
- 3 eggs

Instructions

- Add brown sugar and cinnamon in butter to make a paste.
- Grease the crockpot with butter and transfer half of the butter paste.
- Place the remaining paste on the bread slices. Add the blueberries on top of the bread and layer the other slices on it.
- In a bowl, mix eggs, milk, vanilla and salt. Spoon the egg mixture over the bread and press to let the bread soak thoroughly.
- Cover and let it set at room temperature for 2 hours.
- Place the bread and cook for 4 hours on low.

Nutrients: Kcal: 184, Fats: 17 g, Total Carbs: 30 g, Proteins: 22 g.

26. Breakfast Potatoes

Prep Time: 10 minutes

Cook Time: 5 hours

Servings: 2

Ingredients

- 1 tsp of salt
- 2 tsp of seasoning salt
- 1 tsp of pepper
- 2 tsp of smoked paprika
- 1 onion, diced
- 4 tbsp of garlic butter
- 1 red bell pepper, diced
- 5 oz of potatoes

Instructions

- Add potatoes with onions and bell peppers to the crockpot.
- Add all the seasonings to it and mix. Add garlic butter on top.
- Cook for 3 hours on low until potatoes become tender.

Nutrients: Kcal: 127, Fats: 22 g, Total Carbs: 28 g, Proteins: 16 g.

27. Sausage & Egg Casserole

Prep Time: 20 minutes

Cook Time: 4 hours 20 minutes

Servings: 2

Ingredients

- ½ tsp of salt
- ½ tsp of crushed red pepper flakes
- ¼ tsp of freshly ground black pepper
- 1 cup of shredded Colby cheese
- 1 cup of shredded cheddar cheese
- ½ cup of chopped green onions
- ½ cup of chopped roasted red peppers
- 10 oz of shredded hash brown potatoes
- 10 oz of bulk pork sausage
- 4 eggs

Instructions

- Add foil to the crockpot and grease with butter.
- Season eggs with salt and pepper and beat well. Add cheese and onions in a separate bowl.
- Add potatoes, sausages, roasted pepper and cheese mixture to the pot.
- Spoon the egg mixture, cover and cook for 2-2 ½ hours on low.
- Add cheese on top and cook for 10 more minutes until the cheese melts.

Nutrients: Kcal: 410, Fats: 27 g, Total Carbs: 18 g, Proteins: 23 g.

28. Cheesy Potato Casserole

Prep Time: 15 minutes

Cook Time: 3 hours 15 minutes

Servings: 2

Ingredients

- ½ tsp of salt
- ¼ tsp of black pepper
- 2 tbsp of butter, melted
- ½ cup of chopped onion
- 5 oz of sour cream
- 2 oz of chopped green chiles
- ½ cup of condensed cream of chicken soup
- 1 cup of shredded cheddar cheese
- 5 oz of bacon, cooked and chopped
- 15 oz of shredded hash brown potatoes

Instructions

- Grease the crockpot with butter. Combine all ingredients except hashbrowns and cheese in a large bowl.
- Add hashbrowns and cheese and mix well. Spoon this mixture into the crockpot with some butter.
- Cover with a paper towel and cook on high for 3 hours until it turns brown.

Nutrients: Kcal: 400, Fats: 25 g, Total Carbs: 31 g, Proteins: 13 g.

29. Biscuit & Bacon Casserole

Prep Time: 20 minutes

Cook Time: 2 hours

Servings: 2

Ingredients

- ¼ cup of milk
- ½ medium bell pepper
- 1 medium tomato
- 1 cup of biscuits
- 4 slices of bacon
- 4 large eggs
- 1 cup of shredded cheddar cheese

Instructions

- Add bacon, eggs, cheddar cheese, milk, tomato and bell pepper in a bowl.
- Divide the biscuits into halves. Dip these biscuits in the egg mixture until covered fully.
- Grease the crockpot with butter or oil. Ladle the biscuits and egg mixture into the pot.
- Cook for 2-4 hours on high, until the biscuits and the egg mixture are cooked in the center.

Nutrients: Kcal: 692, Fats: 32 g, Total Carbs: 66 g, Proteins: 26 g.

30. French Toast Casserole

Prep Time: 15 minutes

Cook Time: 4 hours

Servings: 2-4

Ingredients

- ¼ tsp of kosher salt
- ½ cup of brown sugar
- ½ tsp of cinnamon
- ½ tsp of nutmeg
- 1 tsp of vanilla
- 2 cups of milk
- ¼ cup of softened butter
- 1 loaf of gluten-free bread
- 6 large eggs

Instructions

- Add some butter to the crockpot.
- Mix eggs, milk, cinnamon, vanilla, and salt in a large bowl.
- Place the bread into the egg and milk mixture and toss gently.
- Cover and set aside in the refrigerator.
- In another bowl, mix brown sugar, butter, cinnamon and nutmeg.
- Spoon the bread into the crockpot. Season the butter mixture on top and cook for 3 ½ to 4 hours on low.
- Let it cool down for 10-15 minutes before serving.

Nutrients: Kcal: 477, Fats: 18 g, Total Carbs: 63 g, Proteins: 11 g.

31. Hashbrown Sausage Casserole

Prep Time: 20 minutes

Cook Time: 4 hours

Servings: 2

Ingredients

- 1 cup of milk
- ½ tsp of salt
- 1 tsp of sugar
- ¼ tsp of pepper
- ½ tsp of dry mustard
- ½ cup of diced onions
- 1 cup of mozzarella cheese, shredded
- 2 cups of cheddar cheese, shredded
- ½ cup of red bell pepper, diced
- ½ cup of green bell pepper, diced
- 10 oz of frozen hashbrowns
- 5 oz of sausages, cooked
- 5 oz of bacon, cooked
- 8 eggs

Instructions

- Fry the sausages and set them aside. Add bacon to the pan and cook until done.
- In a bowl, beat the eggs with milk, salt, pepper, sugar, and dry mustard.
- Grease the crockpot with oil, add hash browns and layer all the ingredients as desired.
- Spoon the egg and milk mixture, cover and cook for 4 hours on low.

Nutrients: Kcal: 289, Fats: 34 g, Total Carbs: 28 g, Proteins: 4 g.

32. Crockpot Pie

Prep Time: 10 minutes

Cook Time: 3 hours

Servings: 2

Ingredients

- 1 tsp of salt
- 1 tsp of pepper
- 1 tbsp of garlic powder
- 2 tsp of dried basil
- 1 sweet potato
- 1 yellow onion, diced
- 5 oz of pork sausage
- 4 eggs

Instructions

- Grease the pan with coconut oil.
- Put all ingredients in the crockpot and toss well.
- Cook for 2-3 hours on low, until pork becomes tender.

Nutrients: Kcal: 129, Fats: 12 g, Total Carbs: 15 g, Proteins: 6 g.

33. Tex Mex Breakfast

Prep Time: 15 minutes

Cook Time: 2 hours 30 minutes

Servings: 2

Ingredients

- 2 tsp of cilantro
- 1 cup of taco seasoning
- 4 large eggs
- ½ cup of milk
- ½ cup of cheddar cheese, shredded
- 1 cup of hash brown potatoes
- ½ green bell pepper diced
- 1 medium onion diced
- ½ red bell pepper diced
- 1 tsp of green onion
- ¾ cup of ground sausage

Instructions

- Fry the sausage and onions in a pan and set aside.
- Mix eggs, milk and Seasoning mix in a large bowl. Add cheddar cheese.
- Grease the crockpot with butter and layer all the ingredients except the egg mixture.
- Now, spoon the egg mixture into the pot and cook for 2 ½ hours on high until the eggs are set.

Nutrients: Kcal: 205, Fats: 14 g, Total Carbs: 23 g, Proteins: 16 g.

34. Cauliflower Hashbrowns

Prep Time: 10 minutes

Cook Time: 2 hours 30 minutes

Servings: 2

Ingredients

- ½ tsp of salt
- ½ tsp of pepper
- 1 tsp of kosher salt
- ½ tsp of dry mustard
- ½ cup of milk
- 1 small onion, diced
- 2 oz sausages
- 1 cup of shredded cheddar cheese
- ½ head cauliflower shredded
- 4 eggs

Instructions

- Spray the crockpot with some oil.
- Whisk the eggs with milk, dry mustard, salt, and pepper.
- Layer some shredded cauliflower on the bottom of the crockpot, and top with onions. Sprinkle some salt and pepper, along with sausage and cheese.
- Spoon the egg mixture into the crockpot and cook for 2 ½ hours until the top is browned.

Nutrients: Kcal: 197, Fats: 24 g, Total Carbs: 18 g, Proteins: 26 g.

Chapter 9: Beans & Grains

1. Crockpot Beans

Prep Time: 20 minutes

Cook Time: 4-6 hours

Servings: 2

Ingredients

- 1 tsp of kosher salt
- ¼ cup of extra-virgin olive oil
- 10 oz of dried beans

Instructions

- Add beans with all the ingredients and desired seasonings to the crockpot.
- Pour water into the pot.
- Cook for 4-6 hours at low.

Nutrients: Kcal: 45, Fats: 1 g, Total Carbs: 18 g, Proteins: 1.6 g.

2. Pinto Beans

Prep Time: 10 minutes

Cook Time: 6 hours

Servings: 2

Ingredients

- 1 ½ tsp of kosher salt
- 1 tsp of ground cumin
- 1/8 tsp of cayenne pepper
- 1 tsp of dried oregano
- 3 cloves minced garlic
- 2 tsp of extra-virgin olive oil
- 3 cups of water
- 2 bay leaves
- 1 small yellow onion chopped
- 1 jalapeno, chopped
- 4 cups of low-sodium chicken broth
- 2 cups of dry pinto beans

Instructions

- Add the beans to the crockpot.
- In a non-stick pan, heat the oil and add onion and jalapenos with some salt. Cook for 2 minutes, add minced garlic and sauté for 1 more minute.
- Transfer these veggies to the crockpot and add dried seasonings to it.
- Ladle the broth over the beans, cover and cook for 6 hours on high.

Nutrients: Kcal: 131, Fats: 3 g, Total Carbs: 20 g, Proteins: 9 g.

3. Dried Beans

Prep Time: 5 minutes

Cook Time: 6 hours

Servings: 1-2

Ingredients

- ¼ tsp of kosher salt
- ¼ tsp of grounded black pepper
- 1 clove of garlic, minced
- 2-3 cups of water
- 10 oz of dried beans, rinsed, drained

Instructions

- Add garlic, salt, water, beans and pepper to the crockpot.
- Cook for 6 hours on low.

Nutrients: Kcal: 163, Fats: 0.4 g, Total Carbs: 36 g, Proteins: 11 g.

4. Black Forest Ham with Pinto Beans

Prep Time: 15 minutes

Cook Time: 3-4 hours

Servings: 2

Ingredients

- 1 tsp of ground cumin
- 1 tbsp of dried oregano
- 1 tbsp of lard
- 2 large bay leaves
- 3 cloves garlic, chopped
- 1 medium onion, chopped
- ¾ medium green bell pepper, diced
- 5 cups of chicken broth
- 2 medium celery ribs, chopped
- 10 oz of black forest ham
- 10 oz of dried pinto beans

Instructions

- Add water with beans to the crockpot.
- Place the remaining ingredients into the pot and pour chicken broth over it.
- Put the lid on the pot and cook on high for 3-4 hours.

Nutrients: Kcal: 366, Fats: 14 g, Total Carbs: 38 g, Proteins: 28 g.

5. Green Beans, Ham & Potatoes

Prep Time: 30 minutes

Cook Time: 2 hours 45 minutes

Servings: 2

Ingredients

- 1 tsp of seasoning salt
- 1 tsp of black pepper
- 1 tsp of garlic powder
- 1 tsp of onion powder
- 1 tbsp of chicken bouillon granules
- 1 large onion, chopped
- 6 oz of potatoes
- 3 ham hocks
- 6 oz of fresh green beans

Instructions

- Pour water into the beans in the crockpot.
- Add ham hocks and onions, cover and cook for 2 hours at low.
- Take off ham hocks and put potatoes in them.
- Cook for 45 minutes at low. Shred the meat from the ham and discard the bones.
- Season with all seasonings and serve the beans.

Nutrients: Kcal: 200, Fats: 9 g, Total Carbs: 21 g, Proteins: 10 g.

6. Boston Beans

Prep Time: 10 minutes

Cook Time: 2 hours 10 minutes

Servings: 2

Ingredients

- 2 tsp of salt
- ¼ cup of brown sugar
- ¼ tsp of ground black pepper
- 3 tbsp of molasses
- ¼ tsp of dry mustard
- 1 tbsp of Worcestershire sauce
- ½ cup of ketchup
- 1 medium onion, diced
- 1 cup of uncooked bacon strips
- 2 cups of dry navy beans

Instructions

- Add water to soaked navy beans in a pan and boil.

- Lower the heat and cook for 1-2 hours. Drain the excess liquid in a separate container.
- Mix all seasonings with ketchup in a pan and boil.
- Layer the beans in the crockpot and place bacon strips with onions.
- Pour the sauce mixture over the beans and cover with aluminum foil.
- Cook for 1.5 hours at low.

Nutrients: Kcal: 382, Fats: 6 g, Total Carbs: 63 g, Proteins: 21 g.

7. Mexican-Style Pinto Beans

Prep Time: 15 minutes

Cook Time: 4 hours

Servings: 2

Ingredients

- 1 tsp of salt
- 1 tbsp of chili powder
- 1 tbsp of ground cumin
- 1 ½ tsp of garlic powder
- 1 tbsp of cilantro, chopped
- 4 cups of water
- 10 oz of green chili pepper
- 1 yellow onion, chopped
- 1 cup of bacon strips
- 10 oz of dried pinto beans

Instructions

- Add water to the beans in a pot and soak overnight. Drain the water and rinse well.
- Add tomatoes, bacon, onion, chili powder, cumin, and garlic powder to the crockpot.
- Cook for 3 hours at low.
- Add cilantro over it and serve.

Nutrients: Kcal: 267, Fats: 5 g, Total Carbs: 41 g, Proteins: 16 g.

8. Green Bean Casserole

Prep Time: 10 minutes

Cook Time: 2 hours 30 minutes

Servings: 2

Ingredients

- ¼ tsp of salt
- ¼ tsp of ground black pepper
- ⅔ cup of milk
- ½ cup of grated Parmesan cheese
- 3 oz of French-fried onions
- 5 oz of cream of chicken soup
- 8 oz of frozen cut green beans

Instructions

- Add everything to the crockpot.
- Cook at high for about 2 hours and at low for 30 minutes,

Nutrients: Kcal: 272, Fats: 17 g, Total Carbs: 23 g, Proteins: 6 g.

9. Beans with Chicken Fiesta & Rice

Prep Time: 10 minutes

Cook Time: 4 hours

Servings: 2

Ingredients

- 1 cup of uncooked white rice
- 7 oz of tomatoes with green chilies
- 1 oz of chicken taco seasoning mix
- 7 oz of chicken broth
- 10 oz of skinless chicken thighs or breasts
- 7-8 oz of pinto beans

Instructions

- Add everything to the crockpot.

- Cook for 4 hours at high.
- Mix before serving.

Nutrients: Kcal: 327, Fats: 8 g, Total Carbs: 42 g, Proteins: 19 g.

10. Northern White Beans

Prep Time: 15 minutes

Cook Time: 3-4 hours

Servings: 2

Ingredients

- 1 tsp of white sugar
- ½ tsp of soul seasoning
- ½ tsp of white vinegar
- 1 tsp of hot sauce
- ½ onion, finely chopped
- 2 cups of chicken broth
- 2 large smoked neckbones
- 1 ½ cups of dried Northern beans, rinsed & drained

Instructions

- Add broth, seasonings & neck bones to the crockpot. Add soul seasonings and cook for 1 hour at high.
- Once done, shred the meat in a separate bowl.
- Add all other ingredients along with shredded meat to the crockpot.
- Cook for 2-4 hours at high.

Nutrients: Kcal: 252, Fats: 5 g, Total Carbs: 31 g, Proteins: 22 g.

11. Cowboy Beans

Prep Time: 10 minutes

Cook Time: 3 hours

Servings: 3-4

Ingredients

- 1 cup of brown sugar
- 1 cup of ketchup
- 1 tsp of mustard
- 2 onions, chopped
- 7 oz of lima beans
- 7 oz of kidney beans
- 5 oz of bacon
- 10 oz of hamburger
- 14 oz of baked beans with pork

Instructions

- Sauté hamburger and bacon for 7 minutes in a pan.
- Add everything to the crockpot and cook for about 3 hours at low.

Nutrients: Kcal: 471, Fats: 13 g, Total Carbs: 68 g, Proteins: 26 g.

12. Double Beans & Roasted Pepper Chili

Prep Time: 25 minutes

Cook Time: 1 hour 15 minutes

Servings: 2

Ingredients

- 1 tbsp of sweet smoked paprika
- 1 tbsp of dried oregano
- 1 tsp of ground cinnamon
- 2 tbsp of ground cumin
- 1 tbsp of cocoa powder
- 2 celery sticks, chopped
- 2 tbsp of red wine vinegar
- 2 tsp of chipotle paste
- 1 cup of chopped tomatoes
- 2 tbsp of sunflower oil
- 2 onions, chopped
- 2 yellow or orange peppers, chopped
- 1 cup of roasted red peppers

- 1 cup of black beans
- 1 cup of kidney beans
- ½ cup of refried beans

Instructions

- Sauté onions with celery and pepper in oil in a skillet. Drain the excess juice from the peppers.
- Add the chipotle paste, vinegar, cocoa, dried spices and herbs with peppers in a food processor.
- Add refried beans and tomatoes with water and pepper juice to the crockpot. Cook for 1 hour until thickened.
- Add kidney beans and roasted peppers to the pot and cook for 15 minutes. Season before serving.

Nutrients: Kcal: 327, Fats: 6 g, Total Carbs: 41 g, Proteins: 19 g.

13. Kidney Beans Curry

Prep Time: 5 minutes

Cook Time: 3 hours

Servings: 2

Ingredients

- 1 tsp of ground paprika
- 1 tsp of ground cumin
- ½ inch of ginger
- 2 garlic cloves, chopped
- 1 onion, finely chopped
- 1 tbsp of vegetable oil
- 1 cup of cooked rice
- 1 cup of chopped tomatoes
- 1 cup of kidney beans

Instructions

- Sauté onions in the pan. Add ginger, garlic and coriander stalks to the pan, and cook for over 2 minutes.
- Add all spices to the pan and cook for

more than 1 minute.

- Add tomatoes, kidney beans and water to the crockpot and cook at low for 3 hours.
- Season and serve with cooked rice.

Nutrients: Kcal: 282, Fats: 8 g, Total Carbs: 33 g, Proteins: 13 g.

14. Black Bean Chili With Chicken

Prep Time: 10 minutes

Cook Time: 1 hour

Servings: 2

Ingredients

- ½ lime, juiced
- 1 tsp of cumin seeds
- 1 tbsp of oregano
- ½ chicken stock shot
- 3 tbsp of chipotle in adobo
- 2 tbsp of sunflower oil
- 3 garlic cloves, finely chopped
- 2 onions, sliced
- 1 cup of passata
- 1 ½ cups of black beans
- 4 boneless, skinless chicken thighs

Instructions

- Sauté onions in the pan.
- Add everything except passata to the crockpot and cook at low for about 1 hour.
- Once done serve with cooked passata.

Nutrients: Kcal: 256, Fats: 10 g, Total Carbs: 18 g, Proteins: 19 g.

15. White Beans Casserole with Sausages

Prep Time: 20 minutes

Cook Time: 1 hour 5 minutes

Servings: 2

Ingredients

- 2 red onions
- 2 carrots
- 2 tsp of Dijon mustard
- ½ cup of low-salt chicken stock
- 8 chipolatas
- ½ cup of frozen peas
- 1 cup of cherry tomatoes
- 1 red or yellow pepper
- 1 cup of white beans, drained

Instructions

- Add everything to the crockpot and cook at low for about 1.5 hours.
- Serve with rice or desired serving.

Nutrients: Kcal: 367, Fats: 17 g, Total Carbs: 32 g, Proteins: 16 g.

16. Five-Bean Chili

Prep Time: 5 minutes

Cook Time: 30 minutes

Servings: 2

Ingredients

- 1 tsp of sugar
- 2 tsp of hot smoked paprika
- 1 tbsp of ground coriander
- 1 tbsp of ground cumin
- 1 tbsp of coriander, chopped
- 2 garlic cloves, crushed
- 1 onion, sliced
- 2 peppers, sliced

- 1½ tbsp of rapeseed oil
- 1 cup of brown rice
- ½ cup of chopped tomatoes
- ½ cup of black beans, drained
- ½ cup of mixed beans, drained

Instructions

- Add everything to the crockpot and cook at low for about 30 minutes.
- Serve with rice or any desired servings.

Nutrients: Kcal: 438, Fats: 8 g, Total Carbs: 69 g, Proteins: 16 g.

17. Navy Beans & Ham

Prep Time: 10 minutes

Cook Time: 6 hours

Servings: 2

Ingredients

- 1 tsp of kosher salt
- 1 tsp of black pepper
- 1-2 cups of water
- 1 cup of smoked ham
- 10 oz of navy beans, rinsed & drained

Instructions

- Add everything to the crockpot and cook at low for about 6 to 8 hours.

Nutrients: Kcal: 149, Fats: 5 g, Total Carbs: 15 g, Proteins: 11 g.

18. Baked Beans With Maple Syrup

Prep Time: 10 minutes

Cook Time: 6 hours

Servings: 2

Ingredients

- 1 tsp of salt
- ½ tsp of ground pepper
- ½ cup of ketchup

- 1 tbsp of Dijon mustard
- 2 onions
- 3 cups of water
- 1 cup of maple syrup
- ½ cup of streaky salted pork
- 2 cups of dry white beans, rinsed & drained

Instructions

- Add all ingredients to the crockpot. Cook for about 6 hours at low.
- Add seasonings before serving.

Nutrients: Kcal: 457, Fats: 4.7 g, Total Carbs: 80 g, Proteins: 24 g.

19. Brussels Sprouts Grain Bowl

Prep Time: 10 minutes

Cook Time: 3 hours

Servings: 2

Ingredients

- 1 tbsp of olive oil
- 1 tbsp of tahini
- 1 lemon, zested and juiced
- ½ cup of butternut squash
- 2 tsp of maple syrup
- 1-2 tbsp of soft herbs
- 2 tbsp of hummus
- 1 oz of pumpkin seeds
- 1 cup of cooked grains
- 1 cup of brussels sprouts

Instructions

- Add all ingredients to the crockpot. Cook for about 3 hours at low.
- Pour seasonings into the bowls before serving.

Nutrients: Kcal: 628, Fats: 32 g, Total Carbs: 55 g, Proteins: 21 g.

20. Tortellini & Green Beans

Prep Time: 10 minutes

Cook Time: 1 hour

Servings: 2

Ingredients

- ½ tsp of ground black pepper
- 4 cloves garlic minced
- 2 tbsp of vegan butter
- ½ tsp of salt
- 4 oz of French-style frozen green beans
- 2 oz of vegan tortellini

Instructions

- Cook the tortellini as per package directions. Rinse with cold water.
- Add garlic to the melted butter and sauté for 1 minute.
- Stir in green beans with salt and pepper. Mix well and add the beans with tortellini to the crockpot.
- Cook for 1 hour at low.

Nutrients: Kcal: 478, Fats: 16 g, Total Carbs: 64 g, Proteins: 22 g.

21. Barley Risotto Primavera

Prep Time: 20 minutes

Cook Time: 1 hour

Servings: 2

Ingredients

- 1 tsp of salt
- 1 tsp of ground black pepper
- 1 tsp of dried thyme
- 2 tbsp of butter
- 1 tsp of vegetable oil
- 2 tsp of minced garlic
- 1 small onion
- 1 carrot

- 1 zucchini
- ½ cup of grated Parmesan cheese
- 1 cup of pearl barley
- 1 ½ small yellow squash
- 2 cups of chicken broth

Instructions

- Add all ingredients to the crockpot.
- Cook for about 1 hour at low.

Nutrients: Kcal: 297, Fats: 9 g, Total Carbs: 49 g, Proteins: 8 g.

22. Mushroom Lentil Barley

Prep Time: 15 minutes

Cook Time: 4-6 hours

Servings: 2

Ingredients

- 1 tsp of salt
- 2 tsp of ground black pepper
- ¼ cup of dried onion flakes
- 2 tsp of dried summer savory
- 1 tsp of dried basil
- 3 bay leaves
- 2 tsp of minced garlic
- ¾ cup of dry lentils
- 2 cups of vegetable broth
- 2 oz of dried shiitake mushrooms
- 2 cups of sliced button mushrooms
- ¾ cup of uncooked pearl barley

Instructions

- Add all ingredients to the crockpot.
- Cook for about 4 to 6 hours at low.
- Discard the bay leaves before serving.

Nutrients: Kcal: 213, Fats: 1 g, Total Carbs: 44 g, Proteins: 18 g.

23. Barley Chicken Casserole

Prep Time: 15 minutes

Cook Time: 1 hour 20 minutes

Servings: 2

Ingredients

- 1 tsp of dried thyme
- 1 tsp of dried marjoram
- 1 bay leaf, crushed
- 1 tsp of dried parsley
- 1 tsp of ground black pepper
- 1 onion, thinly sliced
- 2 carrots, diced
- 1 green bell pepper, chopped
- 2 ½ cups of chicken stock
- 6 mushrooms
- 2 slices of bacon
- 1 cup of barley
- 2 dark meat chicken pieces

Instructions

- Remove the bacon fat and sauté until browned. Stir in onions and carrots and cook for 2 minutes.
- Add all ingredients to the crockpot.
- Cook for about 1 hour at low.

Nutrients: Kcal: 381, Fats: 11 g, Total Carbs: 44 g, Proteins: 29 g.

24. Barley, Shrimp & Corn Salad

Prep Time: 30 minutes

Cook Time: 1 hour 30 minutes

Servings: 2

Ingredients

- ½ tsp of ground black pepper
- 1 tbsp of chopped fresh thyme
- 1 tsp of minced lemon zest
- ¼ cup of olive oil
- ½ tsp of salt
- 2 ½ cups of water
- ¼ cup of fresh lemon juice
- 4 green onions, chopped
- ½ cup of red bell pepper
- ½ cup of diced green bell pepper
- 1 cup of barley
- 2 cups of corn, thawed
- 10 oz of cooked bay shrimp

Instructions

- Add all ingredients to the crockpot.
- Cook for about 1.5 hour at low.

Nutrients: Kcal: 487, Fats: 17 g, Total Carbs: 56 g, Proteins: 33 g.

25. Barley Mushroom Risotto

Prep Time: 50 minutes

Cook Time: 1 hour

Servings: 2

Ingredients

- 1 tbsp of olive oil
- 1 bay leaf
- 2 garlic, chopped
- ¾ tsp of dried thyme
- 2 tbsp of chopped parsley
- 1 tbsp of butter
- 1 onion, chopped
- 5 cups of chicken broth
- 1 cup of pearl barley
- 10 oz of mushrooms, sliced

Instructions

- Add all ingredients to the crockpot.
- Cook for about 1 hour at low.
- Remove bay leaf and stir barley mixture before serving.

Nutrients: Kcal: 194, Fats: 5 g, Total Carbs: 32 g, Proteins: 7 g.

26. Barley Lentils Pie

Prep Time: 15 minutes

Cook Time: 1 hour

Servings: 2

Ingredients

- 1 tsp of salt
- 1 tsp of pepper
- 1 tsp of all-purpose flour
- 1 tbsp of yeast extract spread
- ½ teaspoon water
- ½ onion, finely chopped
- 1 large carrot, diced
- ½ cup of walnuts, chopped
- 3 potatoes, chopped
- ½ cup of dry lentils
- ¼ cup of pearl barley
- 2 cups of vegetable broth

Instructions

- Add all ingredients to the crockpot.
- Cook for about 1 hour at low.

Nutrients: Kcal: 185, Fats: 5 g, Total Carbs: 30 g, Proteins: 6 g.

27. Mediterranean Barley

Prep Time: 15 minutes

Cook Time: 1 hour

Servings: 2

Ingredients

- 2 cloves of garlic
- ½ cup of chopped cilantro
- 2 ½ cups of water
- 2 tbsp of olive oil
- 1 tbsp of balsamic vinegar
- 4 oz of chopped black olives
- 7 sun-dried tomatoes
- 1 cup of barley

Instructions

- Add all ingredients to the crockpot.
- Cook for about 1 hour at low.
- Stir cilantro and olive oil before serving.

Nutrients: Kcal: 220, Fats: 12 g, Total Carbs: 26 g, Proteins: 4 g.

28. Curried Barley Pilaf

Prep Time: 5 minutes

Cook Time: 1 hour

Servings: 2

Ingredients

- ½ tsp of salt
- ½ tsp of ground allspice
- ½ tsp of ground turmeric
- ¼ tsp of curry powder
- ⅛ tsp of ground black pepper
- 1 onion, diced
- ¼ cup of butter
- ¼ cup of raisins
- ¼ cup of slivered almonds
- 3 ½ cups of chicken broth
- 1 ½ cups of pearl barley

Instructions

- Add all ingredients to the crockpot.
- Cook for about 1 hour at low.
- Add almonds and raisins before serving.

Nutrients: Kcal: 403, Fats: 11 g, Total Carbs: 73 g, Proteins: 7 g.

29. Barley Lime Fiesta

Prep Time: 10 minutes

Cook Time: 1 hour

Servings: 2

Ingredients

- ½ tsp of ground black pepper
- ¼ tsp of onion powder
- 1 tbsp of canola oil
- ½ tsp of salt
- ¼ cup of water
- ½ tsp of ground cumin
- 1 tbsp of lemon juice
- ¼ cup of chopped cilantro
- 1 tsp of distilled white vinegar
- 2 tbsp of light corn syrup
- ¾ tbsp of chipotle pepper in adobo sauce
- 1 stalk of celery, chopped
- ½ green bell pepper, chopped
- 1 large carrot, chopped
- ½ red bell pepper, chopped
- 1 cup of whole-kernel corn
- 1 cup of black beans
- 1 small red onion, chopped
- 1 cup of pearl barley

Instructions

- Add everything to the crockpot and cook for 1 hour at high.

Nutrients: Kcal: 166, Fats: 5 g, Total Carbs: 30 g, Proteins: 4 g.

30. Barley Bake

Prep Time: 25 minutes

Cook Time: 1 hour 40 minutes

Servings: 2

Ingredients

- ¼ tsp of salt
- ⅛ tsp of pepper
- ½ cup of pine nuts
- ½ cup of chopped parsley
- ¼ cup of butter
- 2 green onions, thinly sliced
- 1 medium onion, diced
- 2 cups of vegetable broth
- ½ cup of sliced fresh mushrooms
- 1 cup of uncooked pearl barley

Instructions

- Add all ingredients to the crockpot.
- Cook for about 1 hour and 40 minutes at low.

Nutrients: Kcal: 280, Fats: 14 g, Total Carbs: 33 g, Proteins: 7 g.

Chapter 10: Beef, Pork & Lamb Recipes

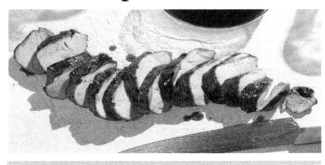

1. Balsamic Pork Tenderloin

Prep Time: 5 minutes

Cook Time: 6 hours

Servings: 2

Ingredients

- 1 tsp of salt
- 1 tsp of pepper
- ½ cup of brown sugar
- 1 tbsp of cornstarch
- ½ cup of water
- 2 tbsp of soy sauce
- ¼ cup of balsamic vinegar
- 12 oz of Pork tenderloin

Instructions

- Combine all spices and seasonings in a bowl.
- Add the balsamic mixture with pork tenderloin to the crockpot.
- Cook for 6 hours on low. Slice the pork tenderloin on a plate.
- Season with desired seasonings before serving.

Nutrients: Kcal: 267, Fats: 8.4 g, Total Carbs: 22 g, Proteins: 8 g.

2. Beef Bourguignon

Prep Time: 20 minutes

Cook Time: 4 hours

Servings: 2

Ingredients

- 3 garlic cloves, chopped
- 1 tbsp of chopped parsley
- 2 tbsp of thyme, chopped
- ¼ cup of flour
- ¼ cup of soy sauce
- ½ cup of tomato sauce
- 2 cups of chicken broth
- 1 cup of red cooking wine
- 2 carrots, sliced
- 4 oz of fresh mushrooms sliced
- 5 oz of baby potatoes
- 3 slices of bacon, chopped
- 8 oz of boneless beef chuck

Instructions

- Sauté bacon in the crockpot. Season with salt and pepper.
- Add beef with broth, red wine, tomato and soy sauce to the crockpot. Cook for 30 minutes on high.
- Add the remaining ingredients to the pot. Cook for 6 hours on low.
- Add chopped parsley before serving.

Nutrients: Kcal: 181, Fats: 8 g, Total Carbs: 22 g, Proteins: 7 g.

3. Pork Carnitas

Prep Time: 10 minutes

Cook Time: 5 hours

Servings: 2

Ingredients

- ¼ cup of lime juice
- 3/4 cup of orange juice
- 1 tsp of salt
- 1 tsp of pepper
- 1 tbsp of chili powder
- 1 tsp of oregano
- 1 tsp of cumin
- 2 cloves of garlic minced
- 1 onion
- 12 oz of pork shoulder roast

Instructions

- Mix all spices in a bowl. Marinate the pork shoulder with all spices.
- Transfer the marinated pork shoulder with the remaining ingredients to the crockpot. Cook for 5 hours on high.
- Shred the pork and cook the sauce for 30 minutes until it thickens.
- Add the pork shoulder to a baking sheet and roast for 5 minutes in the oven.
- Drizzle the prepared sauce over the pork shoulder before serving.

Nutrients: Kcal: 153, Fats: 4 g, Total Carbs: 18 g, Proteins: 7 g.

4. Beer Pot Roast

Prep Time: 15 minutes

Cook Time: 4 hours

Servings: 2

Ingredients

- 1 tsp of kosher salt
- 1 cup of onion soup mix
- 2 tbsp of olive oil
- 3 cloves of garlic, sliced
- 2 tbsp of cornstarch
- 3 tbsp of juices and fat
- 1 tsp of pepper
- 4 large carrots, chopped
- 10 oz of baby or red potatoes
- 1 large yellow onion, sliced
- ¼ cup of water
- 1 ½ cups of beef broth
- 6 oz of beer
- 3-5 chuck roast

Instructions

- Layer half of the onion soup mixed with vegetables in the bottom of the crockpot. Season with salt and pepper.
- Transfer seasoned beef to the crockpot. Cook for 1 hour on low.
- Add beer with the remaining soup mix to the pot and cook for 4 hours on low.

Nutrients: Kcal: 347, Fats: 34 g, Total Carbs: 28 g, Proteins: 16 g.

5. Crockpot Meatloaf

Prep Time: 15 minutes

Cook Time: 6 hours

Servings: 2

Ingredients

- 1/4 cup of brown sugar
- 1 tsp of kosher salt
- ½ tsp of black pepper
- 1 tbsp of yellow mustard
- 6 oz of dried stuffing mix
- 1 ½ cups of ketchup
- 2 tbsp of glaze

- 2 tsp of white vinegar
- 1 ½ cups of whole milk
- 2 large eggs
- 2 tbsp of finely minced onion
- 1 large yellow onion
- 10 oz of ground beef

Instructions

- Combine all ketchup glaze ingredients in a bowl.
- Combine beef with the remaining ingredients and glaze the mixture in the container.
- Transfer the marinated beef mixture to the crockpot. Cook for 6 hours on low.
- Serve with extra glazed sauce.

Nutrients: Kcal: 238, Fats: 36 g, Total Carbs: 47 g, Proteins: 18 g.

6. Port Braised Lamb

Prep Time: 15 minutes

Cook Time: 3 hours

Servings: 2

Ingredients

- 1 tsp of salt
- 1 tsp of pepper
- 2 tsp of dried thyme
- 4 stalks of fresh parsley
- 1 celery stalk, finely chopped
- 3 tbsp of flour
- 3 dried bay leaves
- 3 tbsp of tomato paste
- 2 tbsp of olive oil
- 1 ½ cups of red wine
- 3 cups of port
- 2 cups of beef broth

- 2 garlic cloves, minced
- 1 onion, finely chopped
- 1 carrot, finely chopped
- 4 lamb shanks

Instructions

- Add salt and pepper to the lamb. Fry the lamb shanks in olive oil.
- Cook for 5 minutes on low. Sauté onion with garlic, carrots, and celery in the crockpot with olive oil. Cook for 5 minutes.
- Add flour with the remaining ingredients to the crockpot. Cook for 1 hour on high or 3 hours on low.
- Layer lamb shanks with sauces and serves with mashed potatoes.

Nutrients: Kcal: 203, Fats: 22.5 g, Total Carbs: 18.4 g, Proteins: 60.6 g.

7. Ribeye Steak

Prep Time: 15 minutes

Cook Time: 6 hours

Servings: 2

Ingredients

- 1 tbsp of olive oil
- 1 tsp of salt
- 1 tsp of pepper
- 1 tbsp of onion powder
- 1 large onion, sliced
- 1 cup of onion soup mix
- 2 cups of water
- 6 large baking potatoes, diced
- 10 oz of rib eye

Instructions

- Add salt, onion powder and pepper to the steak.
- Sauté steak on both sides in olive oil

until browned.

- Add steak, onions and potatoes to the crockpot. Cook for 30 minutes.
- Add onion soup mix with water to the crockpot. Cook for 6 hours on low.

Nutrients: Kcal: 222.4, Fats: 4.8 g, Total Carbs: 15.5 g, Proteins: 28.1 g.

8. Pepper Steak

Prep Time: 15 minutes

Cook Time: 6 hours

Servings: 2

Ingredients

- ½ tsp of kosher salt
- ¼ tsp of red pepper flakes
- ½ tsp of black pepper
- 2 tsp of garlic powder
- 5 tbsp of cornstarch
- 2 tbsp of honey
- ¼ cup of water
- 1 tbsp of canola oil, grapeseed oil
- 2 tbsp of Worcestershire sauce
- ¼ cup of low-sodium soy sauce
- 1 tbsp of minced fresh ginger
- 1 large yellow onion
- 1 red or orange bell pepper
- 1 green bell pepper
- 5 oz of roasted tomatoes
- 10 oz of sirloin
- 1 cup of cooked brown rice quinoa

Instructions

- Season beef with salt, pepper and garlic powder.
- Sauté beef from both sides in olive oil for 5 minutes.
- Add beef with all ingredients, except

sauces, to the crockpot. Cook for 2 hours on low.

- Add all sauces to the pot and cook for 1 hour on low.
- Add chopped spring onions and serve with cooked brown rice.

Nutrients: Kcal: 396, Fats: 11 g, Total Carbs: 28 g, Proteins: 36 g.

9. Crock Pot Beef Stew

Prep Time: 20 minutes

Cook Time: 4 hours

Servings: 2

Ingredients

- 3 tbsp of flour
- 1 tsp of dried rosemary
- 1 cup of celery stalks
- ½ tsp of garlic powder
- ½ tsp of thyme
- 2 tbsp of cornstarch
- 1 tbsp of Worcestershire sauce
- 1 cup of vegetable juice
- 3 tbsp of olive oil
- 2 tbsp of water
- 4 cups of beef broth
- 1 onion chopped
- ¾ cup of peas
- 2 cups of carrots
- 1 ½ cups of potatoes, cubed
- 10 oz of beef chuck or stewing beef

Instructions

- Marinate beef with all spices in a bowl.
- Cook beef for 4-5 hours on low until browned.
- Add peas and cornstarch with water to the crockpot.

- Cook for 1 hour on low and season with salt and pepper before serving.

Nutrients: Kcal: 480, Fats: 24 g, Total Carbs: 29 g, Proteins: 36 g.

10. Ranch Pork Chops

Prep Time: 5 minutes

Cook Time: 6 hours

Servings: 2

Ingredients

- ¼ tsp of pepper
- ½ tsp of dried thyme
- 1 tbsp of thyme, chopped
- 1 tbsp of minced, fresh garlic
- 1 tsp of cornstarch
- 1 cup of dry Ranch salad dressing
- 10 oz of condensed cream of chicken soup
- 6 pork chops

Instructions

- Mix all ingredients and transfer to the greased crockpot.
- Cook for 6 hours on low.
- Add chopped parsley on top before serving.

Nutrients: Kcal: 280, Fats: 7.7 g, Total Carbs: 7.2 g, Proteins: 28.8 g.

11. Lamb Shoulder

Prep Time: 20 minutes

Cook Time: 3 hours

Servings: 2

Ingredients

- 1 tsp of salt
- 1 tsp of pepper
- 4 tbsp of corn flour
- 1 tsp of blackcurrant jam
- 4 sprigs of rosemary
- 4 garlic cloves sliced
- 1 onion chopped
- 1 carrot chopped
- 1 ½ cups of red wine
- 2 cups of lamb stock
- 12 oz of lamb shoulder

Instructions

- Mix all vegetables with sprigs of rosemary and corn flour.
- Season lamb with salt and pepper.
- Transfer the vegetables and lamb to the crockpot. Cook for 3 hours on low.
- Place the lamb on foil paper and roast in the oven for 20-30 minutes.
- Drizzle the gravy over the lamb and serve.

Nutrients: Kcal: 371, Fats: 11 g, Total Carbs: 13 g, Proteins: 44 g.

12. Pork Vindaloo

Prep Time: 15 minutes

Cook Time: 5 hours

Servings: 2

Ingredients

- 1 tsp of sea salt
- ⅛ tsp of red pepper flakes
- 1 ½ tbsp of cumin
- 2 tbsp of curry powder
- ½ tsp of ground cloves
- 1 ½ tsp of cardamom
- 3 tbsp of mustard seeds
- 1 cinnamon stick
- 1 tbsp of chopped cilantro
- 2 tbsp of ginger, grated
- 6 cloves garlic

- ¼ cup of olive oil
- ½ cup of white wine vinegar
- 1 onion, sliced
- 2 tomatoes
- 2 red peppers, sliced
- 1 cup of cooked rice
- 10 oz of pork loin or pork shoulder, cubed

Instructions

- Blend all spices with olive oil in a food processor.
- Layer onions and peppers in the bottom of the crockpot.
- Add cubed pork with prepared puree and remaining seasonings to the crockpot.
- Cook on low for 4-5 hours.
- Top with chopped cilantro and serve with cooked rice.

Nutrients: Kcal: 347, Fats: 34 g, Total Carbs: 28 g, Proteins: 16 g.

13. Braised Lamb Ragu

Prep Time: 15 minutes

Cook minutes: 3 hours

Servings: 2

Ingredients

- 1 tsp of kosher salt
- 1 tsp of black pepper
- 6 sprigs of fresh thyme
- 1 sprig of fresh rosemary
- 1 stalk celery, finely diced
- 2 bay leaves
- 2 tbsp of olive oil
- 6 cloves garlic, chopped
- 2 tbsp of tomato paste

- 1 cup of dry red wine
- 1 cup of low-sodium beef stock
- 1 yellow onion, finely diced
- 2 carrots, finely diced
- 12 oz of crushed tomatoes
- 10-12 oz of lamb shoulder

Instructions

- Season lamb with salt and pepper.
- Sauté seasoned lamb for 2-3 minutes on both sides.
- Add all veggies and spices to the crockpot and cook for 5 minutes.
- Add fried lamb to the crockpot and cook for 3-4 hours on low.
- Discard the bay leaves before serving.

Nutrients: Kcal: 315, Fats: 16 g, Total Carbs: 17 g, Proteins: 28 g.

14. Honey Pork Chops

Prep Time: 5 minutes

Cook Time: 4 hours

Servings: 2

Ingredients

- 2 garlic cloves chopped
- 2 tbsp of corn flour
- 1 tbsp of chopped parsley
- 4 tbsp of soy sauce
- ½ cup of tomato ketchup
- ¼ cup of honey
- 4 Pork chops

Instructions

- Combine all ingredients, except pork chops, in the food processor. Blend well until puree.
- Drizzle the sauce over the pork chops and transfer to the crockpot.

- Cook for 4 hours on low.
- Add the cornstarch mixture to the pot until the sauce is thickened.
- Add chopped parsley on top.

Nutrients: Kcal: 338, Fats: 9 g, Total Carbs: 31 g, Proteins: 31 g.

15. Pork Loin

Prep Time: 30 minutes

Cook Time: 5 hours

Servings: 2

Ingredients

- 1 tbsp of honey
- 1 tbsp of Dijon mustard
- 3 sprigs of thyme
- 2 garlic cloves
- 1½ tsp of fennel seeds
- 2 tbsp of olive oil
- 2 apples
- ½ cup of shallots
- 1 cup of white wine
- ½ cup of chicken or pork stock
- 10 oz of pork loin

Instructions

- Add all spices to a bowl. Coat the pork loin with all spices and rest at room temperature.
- Add shallots to the boiling water and cook for 2 minutes.
- Transfer the pork loins to the crockpot. Cook for 4-6 hours on low.
- Place the pork loin on a foil and roast for 10 minutes in the oven.
- Serve with mashed potatoes and roasted veggies.

Nutrients: Kcal: 597, Fats: 41 g, Total Carbs: 9 g, Proteins: 42 g.

16. Lamb Roast

Prep Time: 30 minutes

Cook Time: 6 hours

Servings: 2-4

Ingredients

- 2 tsp of salt
- ½ tsp of pepper
- 1 tbsp of oregano
- 2 tsp of rosemary leaves
- 4 potatoes, chopped
- 2 onions, chopped
- 2 tsp of garlic, crushed
- 1 tsp of garlic
- 2 carrots, chopped
- ½ cup of chicken stock
- 10-12 oz of the leg of lamb

Instructions

- Add salt, pepper, and garlic to the lamb.
- Fry the lamb from both sides in some oil.
- Add seasoned lamb with all veggies and spices to the crockpot.
- Cook for 6 hours on high.

Nutrients: Kcal: 437, Fats: 27.6 g, Total Carbs: 39 g, Proteins: 39 g.

17. Moroccan Lamb with Apricots

Prep Time: 10 minutes

Cook Time: 4 hours

Servings: 2

Ingredients

- 1 tsp of brown sugar
- 1 tsp of salt
- 1 tsp of ground cumin
- 1 tsp of turmeric
- 1 tsp of cinnamon
- 2 tbsp of flour
- 1 tsp of ground ginger
- 1 tsp of ground coriander
- 1 cup of yogurt
- 1 cup of beef stock
- 1 onion, sliced
- 1 cup of crushed tomatoes
- 1 carrot, chopped
- 1 cup of chickpeas
- ½ cup of dried apricots, chopped
- 10 oz of lamb chops, shanks

Instructions

- Place all ingredients in the crockpot.
- Cook for 2 hours on high or 6 hours on low.
- Add salt and pepper to the crockpot before serving.
- Serve with burritos or cooked rice.

Nutrients: Kcal: 347, Fats: 16 g, Total Carbs: 20 g, Proteins: 48 g.

18. Minced Beef

Prep Time: 5 minutes

Cook Time: 4 hours

Servings: 2

Ingredients

- 1 tsp of salt
- 1 red chili, sliced
- 1 tbsp ground allspice
- 2 tsp of turmeric
- 1 tsp of pepper
- 2 tsp of coriander
- 1 tsp of ginger
- 2 cloves garlic, sliced
- 2 onions, chopped
- ½ cup of frozen green peas
- 2 large potatoes, chopped
- 1 cup of chopped tomatoes
- 10 oz of minced beef

Instructions

- Combine all spices with tomato in a bowl.
- Add all ingredients, except frozen peas, to the crockpot.
- Cook for 2 hours on high or 6 hours on low.
- Add peas to the pot and cook for 30 minutes.
- Top with chopped spinach before serving.

Nutrients: Kcal: 304, Fats: 42 g, Total Carbs: 69 g, Proteins: 42 g.

19. Sauerkraut & Pork

Prep Time: 10 minutes

Cook Time: 4 hours

Servings: 2

Ingredients

- 1 tsp of kosher salt
- 1 tbsp of brown sugar
- ½ tsp of ground black pepper
- 2 large bay leaves
- 2 tsp of caraway seeds
- 1 large onion
- 1 apple
- ½ cup of apple juice
- 1 cup of sauerkraut
- 10 oz of pork roast loin

Instructions

- Season pork with salt and pepper.
- Layer pork and sauerkraut in the crockpot.
- Add all ingredients to the pot and cook on high for 4 hours. Slice it before serving.
- Discard the bay leaves before serving and add chopped parsley to them.

Nutrients: Kcal: 394, Fats: 10 g, Total Carbs: 16 g, Proteins: 56 g.

20. Smoky Barbecue Pork Ribs

Prep Time: 15 minutes

Cook Time: 4 hours

Servings: 2

Ingredients

- 1 tsp of garlic powder
- 1 tbsp of ground cumin
- 2 tsp of dried oregano
- 1 tbsp of smoked paprika
- 1/3 cup of golden syrup
- ½ cup of barbecue sauce
- 1/3 cup of sauce
- 2 tbsp of Italian white wine vinegar
- 10 oz of pork ribs

Instructions

- Mix all ingredients in a container.
- Add ribs and sauces to the crockpot. Cook for 4 hours on low or 2 hours on high.
- Wrap ribs with foil paper and roast in the oven for 10 minutes.
- Drizzle the prepared sauce on top and serve.

Nutrients: Kcal: 347, Fats: 39 g, Total Carbs: 38 g, Proteins: 72 g.

21. Spiced Orange Lamb

Prep Time: 15 minutes

Cook Time: 6 hours

Servings: 2

Ingredients

- 1 cup of salt reduced chicken style liquid stock
- 1 tbsp of grated orange rind
- ½ cup of orange juice
- 2 tbsp of honey
- 1 tbsp of ground cumin
- 10 oz of butterflied legs of lamb

Instructions

- Combine all ingredients in the bowl.
- Coat lamb with the prepared mixture.
- Transfer the marinated lamb pieces to the crockpot.
- Cook for 6 hours on low until tender.

Nutrients: Kcal: 430, Fats: 27 g, Total Carbs: 9 g, Proteins: 36 g.

22. Eggplant, Tomatoes & Basil Beef

Prep Time: 15 minutes

Cook Time: 6 hours

Servings: 2

Ingredients

- 2 tbsp of plain flour
- 2 tbsp of olive oil
- ½ cup of fresh basil leaves
- 2 tbsp of tomato paste
- 1 ½ cups of chopped tomatoes
- ½ cup of red wine
- 1 onion, chopped
- 1 eggplant
- 1 zucchini
- 2/3 cup of beef stock
- 1 cup of gravy beef

Instructions

- Rub beef with flour and toss well to combine.
- Add beef to the crockpot and cook until browned.
- Add all the remaining ingredients to the crockpot and cook for 6 hours on low.
- Serve with polenta and top with basil leaves.

Nutrients: Kcal: 325, Fats: 15 g, Total Carbs: 34 g, Proteins: 13 g.

23. Thai Pork Curry

Prep Time: 10 minutes

Cook Time: 4 hours

Servings: 2

Ingredients

- 2-star anise
- 2 tbsp of brown sugar
- 1 tsp of Chicken stock powder
- 2 tbsp of tamarind paste
- ½ cup of Thai red curry paste
- 1 ½ cups of coconut milk
- 1-2 tbsp of ginger, sliced
- 2 garlic cloves, bruised
- 2 bunches of broccolini
- 2 bunches of gai larn
- 2 lemongrass stalks
- 2 tsp of peanut oil
- ½ cup of dried shiitake mushrooms
- 10 oz of boneless pork leg

Instructions

- Sauté pork from both sides in some oil for 8-10 minutes on low.
- Mix coconut milk with stock powder, sugar, tamarind and curry paste in a bowl and blend well.
- Add the prepared mixture with the remaining ingredients and pork to the crockpot.
- Cook for 4 hours on low. Sauté gai larn and broccolini in a separate pan.
- Drain the excess water and add it to the crockpot.
- Serve with cooked rice.

Nutrients: Kcal: 488, Fats: 21 g, Total Carbs: 20 g, Proteins: 54 g.

24. Lamb Chili

Prep Time: 10 minutes

Cook Time: 4 hours 40 minutes

Servings: 2-4

Ingredients

- 1 red onion, diced
- 2 tbsp of garlic, minced
- 1 cup of pinto beans, rinsed & drained

- 1/2 cup of chili seasoning
- 4 tbsp of taco sauce
- 1 cup of medium salsa
- 1 cup of black beans, rinsed & drained
- 1 cup of corn
- 1 cup of diced tomatoes
- 1 cup of cannellini beans, rinsed & drained
- 1 cup of red wine
- 1 cup of red kidney beans, rinsed & drained
- 2 tbsp of olive oil
- 10 oz of ground lamb

Instructions

- Sauté lamb with onions and garlic in olive oil.
- Add the remaining ingredients with sautéed lamb to the crockpot.
- Cook for 4-6 hours on low. Shred cheddar cheese before serving.

Nutrients: Kcal: 240, Fats: 5 g, Total Carbs: 27 g, Proteins: 15 g.

25. Shredded Beef Tacos

Prep Time: 15 minutes

Cook Time: 6 hours

Servings: 2

Ingredients

- 1 tbsp of salt
- 1 tbsp of pepper
- 2 tbsp of olive oil
- 1 tbsp of paprika
- 2 tsp of chili powder
- 1 tsp of cumin
- 1 tsp of garlic powder
- 1 tbsp of chipotle powder
- ¼ cup of lime juice
- 2 cups of beef broth
- 1 white onion, sliced
- 4-6 flour tortillas
- 10 oz of chuck steak, boneless

Instructions

- Season beef with salt and pepper. Fry the beef from both sides in olive oil for 5 minutes.
- Add the remaining ingredients with beef to the crockpot. Cook for 2 hours on high or 8 hours on low.
- Shred the beef on a plate.
- Assemble the tacos with desired toppings and seasonings.

Nutrients: Kcal: 487, Fats: 12 g, Total Carbs: 20 g, Proteins: 36 g.

26. Beef Teriyaki Steak Bites

Prep Time: 10 minutes

Cook Time: 4 hours

Servings: 2

Ingredients

- ¼ cup of brown sugar
- 1/4 cup of honey
- 1 cup of water
- 1 tsp of black pepper
- 1 tbsp of sesame oil
- 1 ½ cups of soy sauce
- 1 tbsp of white sesame seeds
- 1 tbsp of ginger, minced
- 2 tbsp of garlic, minced
- 2 tbsp of cornstarch
- 10 oz of Sirloin steak

Instructions

- Mix all spices in the bowl.
- Add sirloin with sauce to the crockpot. Cook for 3 hours on low.
- Add cornstarch with water to the pot until it thickens.
- Season green onions and sesame seeds before serving.
- Serve with cooked rice or burritos.

Nutrients: Kcal: 271, Fats: 14 g, Total Carbs: 22 g, Proteins: 31 g.

27. Pulled Lamb Birria Tacos

Prep Time: 15 minutes

Cook Time: 6 hours

Servings: 2

Ingredients

- 1 tbsp of vegetable oil
- 5 oz of pork shoulder
- 1 onion sliced
- 1 cup of crushed tomatoes
- 10 oz of light beer
- 1-2 tbsp of chipotle paste
- 1 tsp of cracked coriander seeds
- ½ tsp of cinnamon
- ½ tsp of nutmeg
- 1 tbsp of cumin
- 1 dry ancho chili
- 1 bay leaf
- 1 tbsp of oregano
- 3 garlic cloves sliced
- 2 tsp of corn flour
- 1 tsp of salt

Instructions

- Sauté onions for 2-4 minutes in the crockpot.
- Add all spices to the pot and cook for 3-4 minutes.
- Add lamb to the pot and cook for 6 hours on low.
- Add salt with cornstarch mixture to the crockpot until thickened. Cook for 15 minutes.
- Serve with desired toppings and tacos.

Nutrients: Kcal: 465, Fats: 35 g, Total Carbs: 9 g, Proteins: 25 g.

28. Lamb Stew with Potatoes

Prep Time: 10 minutes

Cook Time: 4 hours

Servings: 2

Ingredients

- 1 tsp of dried oregano
- 1 tsp of ground cinnamon
- 3 bay leaves
- 2 celery sticks, chopped
- 2 onions, sliced
- 4 garlic cloves
- 4 tbsp of red wine vinegar
- 2 potatoes
- 1 cup of chopped tomatoes
- 3 tbsp of tomato purée
- 10 oz of lamb shoulder, diced

Instructions

- Add all ingredients with lamb to the crockpot.
- Cook for 6 hours on low.
- Season with herbs and serve with cooked rice.

Nutrients: Kcal: 330, Fats: 12 g, Total Carbs: 20 g, Proteins: 33 g.

29. Pork Adobo

Prep Time: 30 minutes

Cook Time: 6 hours

Servings: 2

Ingredients

- 1 tsp of salt
- 1 tsp of white sugar
- 6 dried bay leaves
- ½ cup of soy sauce
- 1 tbsp of oyster sauce
- ¼ cup of apple cider vinegar
- 1 tbsp of minced garlic
- 1 ½ cups of beef broth
- 6 hard-boiled eggs
- 2 tsp of the whole peppercorn
- 4 pork shoulder sliced

Instructions

- Mix all the ingredients in a container and blend well. Let it marinate for 30 minutes.
- Add all ingredients with beef broth to the crockpot.
- Cook for 5 hours on high.
- Add boiled eggs, salt and vinegar half an hour before serving.

Nutrients: Kcal: 347, Fats: 34 g, Total Carbs: 28 g, Proteins: 16 g.

30. Beef Joint

Prep Time: 15 minutes

Cook Time: 3 hours 45 minutes

Servings: 2

Ingredients

- ½ tbsp of flaked sea salt
- 1 tsp of ground black pepper
- ½ tbsp of mustard powder
- 2 tbsp of wholegrain mustard
- 2-4 tbsp of plain flour
- 2 tbsp of butter
- 1 garlic clove, crushed
- 2 onions, sliced
- 1 carrot, sliced
- ½ tbsp of chopped rosemary leaves
- 6 oz of beef stock
- 4-5 beef roasting joint

Instructions

- Mix all spices in a bowl. Marinate the beef with an allspice mixture.
- Layer carrots and onions at the bottom of the crockpot. Place beef on top of vegetables.
- Ladle broth in it. Cook for 3 hours on low.
- Wrap the beef in foil paper and rest at room temperature for 10 minutes.
- Discard the vegetables from the crockpot.
- Cook the broth with butter for 45 minutes on low.
- Slice the beef and serve with prepared gravy.

Nutrients: Kcal: 444, Fats: 26 g, Total Carbs: 9 g, Proteins: 43 g.

Chapter 11: Poultry

1. Cajun Chicken Alfredo

Prep Time: 15 minutes

Cook Time: 2 hours 30 minutes

Servings: 2

Ingredients

- 1 tsp of kosher salt
- 1 tsp of black pepper
- 1 tsp of garlic powder
- 2 tbsp of Cajun seasoning
- 2 tbsp of butter
- 1 tbsp of olive oil
- ½ cup of heavy cream
- 2 cloves garlic, chopped
- ½ cup of hot water
- 5 oz of smoked sausage
- 2 cups of low-sodium chicken broth
- 2 cups of shredded parmesan cheese
- 5 oz of uncooked penne pasta
- 5 oz of chicken breasts

Instructions

- Season chicken with salt, garlic powder and pepper. Sauté chicken in olive oil in the crockpot.
- Add the remaining ingredients to the pot. Cook for 4 hours on low until chicken becomes tender.
- Slice the chicken on a plate. Add penne pasta to the crockpot and cook for 30 minutes.
- Add parmesan cheese and sliced chicken when the pasta is done.

Nutrients: Kcal: 528, Fats: 64 g, Total Carbs: 49 g, Proteins: 38 g.

2. Sticky Chicken

Prep Time: 10 minutes

Cook Time: 4 hours

Servings: 2

Ingredients

- ⅓ cup of coconut sugar
- 1 tsp of black pepper freshly ground
- 1 tsp of ginger powder
- 1 tsp of onion powder
- 2-4 tbsp of cornstarch
- ¼ cup of honey
- ⅓ cup of balsamic vinegar
- 2 tsp of Sriracha sauce
- ⅓ cup of tamari soy sauce
- 3 cloves garlic, minced
- 1 tbsp of water
- 10 oz chicken thighs

Instructions

- Combine all ingredients with chicken in the crockpot, except cornstarch water.
- Cook for 3-4 hours on low.
- Add cornstarch with water over the chicken to thicken the sauce.
- Cook for 15 minutes, add desired seasonings and serve.

Nutrients: Kcal: 247, Fats: 16 g, Total Carbs: 13 g, Proteins: 16 g.

3. Satay Chicken

Prep Time: 15 minutes

Cook Time: 2 hours 30 minutes

Servings: 2

Ingredients

- 1 tbsp of fresh mint leaves
- 1 tbsp of fresh coriander leaves
- 2 garlic cloves, finely chopped
- 3 tsp of grated fresh ginger
- 1 small red onion, chopped
- ½ cup of coconut cream
- ½ cup of smooth peanut butter
- 2 tbsp of kecap manis
- 5 oz of chicken thigh cutlets, trimmed

Instructions

- Fry seasoned chicken cutlets in a crockpot for 5-10 minutes on low.
- Sauté garlic and ginger in the pot.
- Add chicken with the remaining ingredients to the pot and cook for 4 hours on low.
- Garnish with chopped cilantro. Serve with rice or tortilla.

Nutrients: Kcal: 151, Fats: 4.68 g, Total Carbs: 15.67 g, Proteins: 5.65 g.

4. Spiced Chicken

Prep Time: 10 minutes

Cook Time: 3 hours

Servings: 2

Ingredients

- 1/2 tsp of kosher salt
- 1/4 tsp of black pepper
- 1-2 tsp of granulated sugar
- ½ tsp of smoked paprika
- ½ tsp of ground turmeric
- ¼ tsp of ground cumin
- 2 tbsp of fresh cilantro minced
- 1 tbsp of fresh ginger grated
- 3 cloves minced garlic
- 2 tbsp of tomato paste
- 1 cup of tomato sauce
- 3 tbsp of vegetable oil
- 3/4 cup of whole-fat plain yogurt
- 1 medium yellow onion minced
- 1 serrano pepper
- 10 oz of boneless, skinless chicken thighs

Instructions

- Add seasoned chicken to the crockpot.
- Sauté chicken for 5 minutes. Slice the chicken on a plate.
- Add onions with remaining spices to the crockpot. Sauté for 4-5 minutes.
- Stir in ginger and garlic and cook for 1-2 minutes.
- Add sliced chicken with tomatoes to the crockpot. Cook for 3 hours on low.
- Add yogurt to the pot and cook for 5 minutes.
- Season with cilantro on top before serving.

Nutrients: Kcal: 347, Fats: 34 g, Total Carbs: 28 g, Proteins: 16 g.

5. Sticky Chicken with Noodles

Prep Time: 30 minutes

Cook Time: 2 hours

Servings: 2

- **Ingredients**
- 1 tbsp of brown sugar
- 1-2 tbsp of flour
- 3 tbsp of honey
- ¾ cup of cup soy sauce
- 1 small onion
- 3 cloves of garlic
- 1 tsp of sesame seeds
- 2 tbsp of spring onions
- 8 oz chicken, cubed

Instructions

- Add flour to the chicken. Sauté onions in the crockpot.
- Add all remaining ingredients along with the chicken to the pot.
- Cook for 2 hours on low.
- Season with fried onions and serve with cooked rice.

Nutrients: Kcal: 147, Fats: 23 g, Total Carbs: 9.8 g, Proteins: 14 g.

6. Honey Bourbon Chicken

Prep Time: 5 minutes

Cook Time: 3 hours

Servings: 2

Ingredients

- ½ tsp of red chili flakes
- 1 cup of honey
- 4 tbsp of vegetable oil
- ½ cup of ketchup
- 1 cup of low-sodium soy sauce
- ½ cup of diced onion
- 1 tsp of minced garlic
- 8 oz of boneless skinless chicken breasts

Instructions

- Add chicken to the crockpot.
- Add all the ingredients to a bowl and mix well.
- Spoon the prepared sauce mixture over the chicken.
- Cook on low for 3-4 hours or 1-2 hours on high.
- Slice the chicken before serving.

Nutrients: Kcal: 315, Fats: 20 g, Total Carbs: 41 g, Proteins: 52 g.

7. Chicken Alfredo

Prep Time: 15 minutes

Cook Time: 3 hours 30 minutes

Servings: 2

Ingredients

- 1 tsp of kosher salt
- 1 tsp of black pepper
- 1 tsp of garlic powder
- 2 tbsp of Cajun seasoning
- 3 cups of heavy cream
- 1 tbsp of olive oil
- 4 tbsp of butter
- ½ cup of hot water
- 2 cloves garlic, minced
- 4 cups of low-sodium chicken broth
- 10 oz of uncooked penne pasta
- 2 cups of shredded parmesan cheese
- 10 oz of smoked sausage
- 10 oz of chicken breasts

Instructions

- Season chicken with spices. Cook chicken in olive oil from both sides in the crockpot.
- Add sausages, heavy cream, garlic, Cajun seasonings and chicken broth to the crockpot.
- Cook for 3-4 hours on high. Slice the chicken on a plate.
- Stir in penne pasta in hot water.
- Cook for 30 minutes, until the pasta is done.
- Top the pasta with sliced chicken and parmesan cheese.

Nutrients: Kcal: 267, Fats: 64 g, Total Carbs: 48 g, Proteins: 39 g.

8. Mississippi Chicken

Prep Time: 5 minutes

Cook Time: 6 hours

Servings: 2

Ingredients

- ½ cup of salted butter
- ¼ cup of ranch dressing mix
- ½ cup of au jus gravy mix
- 6 pepperoncini peppers
- 3 boneless, skinless chicken breasts

Instructions

- Season chicken with gravy mix and ranch dressing.
- Add seasoned chicken with butter and pepperoncini to the crockpot.
- Cook for 6 hours on low. Shred the chicken on a plate.

Nutrients: Kcal: 210, Fats: 11 g, Total Carbs: 3 g, Proteins: 28 g.

9. Garden Chicken Pasta

Prep Time: 5 minutes

Cook Time: 4 hours

Servings: 2

Ingredients

- ¼ tsp of black pepper
- 8 oz of olive garden Italian dressing
- ¼ cup of parmesan cheese
- 4 oz of cream cheese
- 8 oz of penne pasta, cooked
- 10 oz of boneless skinless chicken breast

Instructions

- Add chicken with all ingredients to the crockpot. Add cream cheese on top.
- Cook for 4 hours on low.
- Place the cream cheese on top. Cook for 4 hours on low.
- Add drained pasta with sauce to the crockpot.
- Season with parmesan cheese and serve.

Nutrients: Kcal: 267, Fats: 9 g, Total Carbs: 41 g, Proteins: 13 g.

10. White Chicken Chili

Prep Time: 15 minutes

Cook Time: 3 hours

Servings: 2

Ingredients

- ½ tsp of kosher salt
- 1 tsp of dried oregano
- 1 tsp of ground cumin
- ¼ cup of chopped fresh cilantro
- ¼ tsp of cayenne pepper
- 1 small yellow onion

- 2 cloves garlic minced
- 1 cup of diced green chiles
- 4 cups of low-sodium chicken stock
- 1 cup of low-sodium white beans
- 4 boneless skinless chicken breasts

Instructions

- Add all ingredients with chicken breasts to the crockpot.
- Cook for 4-6 hours on low. Remove the chicken from the pot.
- Blend the mixture of the crockpot in a blender until puree.
- Add chicken with prepared sauce in a bowl.
- Season with parmesan cheese and cilantro.

Nutrients: Kcal: 216, Fats: 4 g, Total Carbs: 36 g, Proteins: 34 g.

11. Pineapple Chicken Rice Bowl

Prep Time: 15 minutes

Cook Time: 2 hours 50 minutes

Servings: 2

Ingredients

- ½ cup of honey
- 1 tsp of salt
- 2 tsp of black pepper
- 2 tsp of fresh ginger, grated
- 1 tbsp of fresh garlic, minced
- ½ Poblano pepper, minced
- ¼ cup of butter
- 1-2 tsp of Asian chili garlic sauce
- ½ cup of tamari sauce
- 2 cups of pineapple juice
- 1/3 cup of apple cider vinegar
- 2-4 boneless skinless chicken breasts

Instructions

- Add chicken with all sauce ingredients to the crockpot, except corn starch.
- Cook for 2 hours on low. Remove the chicken from a plate.
- Add corn starch mixture to the crockpot. Cook for 10-15 minutes on low.
- Cook rice in the crockpot with pineapple juice.
- Add pineapple chicken rice to a bowl and serve.

Nutrients: Kcal: 250, Fats: 6 g, Total Carbs: 26 g, Proteins: 6 g.

12. Cool Ranch Chicken

Prep Time: 10 minutes

Cook Time: 6 hours

Servings: 2

Ingredients

- ½ cup of dry ranch dressing mix
- ¼ cup of dry taco mix
- 1 ½ cups of low-sodium chicken broth
- 2 boneless skinless chicken breasts

Instructions

- Add all ingredients to the crockpot.
- Cook for 6 hours on low. Shred the chicken before serving.
- Serve with burritos or tortillas.

Nutrients: Kcal: 217, Fats: 21 g, Total Carbs: 34 g, Proteins: 26 g.

13. Angel Chicken

Prep Time: 10 minutes

Cook Time: 6 hours

Servings: 2

Ingredients

- ¼ cup of butter
- 3 cloves garlic, chopped
- 2 tbsp of Italian dressing mix
- 4 oz of cream cheese
- 10 oz of cream of chicken soup
- ¾ cup of chicken stock
- 10 oz of angel hair pasta
- 10 oz of chicken breast, boneless and skinless

Instructions

- Grease the crockpot with some oil. Add chicken with garlic to the crockpot.
- Combine all ingredients in a container and mix well. Spoon this mixture over the chicken.
- Cook for 6 hours on low.
- Cook the angel hair pasta as per directions. Slice the chicken before serving.

Nutrients: Kcal: 208, Fats: 11 g, Total Carbs: 44 g, Proteins: 29 g.

14. Creamy Italian Chicken

Prep Time: 10 minutes

Cook Time: 4 hours

Servings: 2-4

Ingredients

- 1 tsp of black pepper
- 1 tsp of parsley, chopped
- 2 tbsp of Zesty Italian dressing mix
- 8 oz of low-fat cream cheese, cubed
- ½ cup of milk
- 2 cups of fat-free cream of chicken soup
- 10 oz of boneless skinless chicken breasts

Instructions

- Add seasoned chicken breasts to the greased crockpot.
- Spoon cream of chicken soup with Italian dressing mix over the chicken.
- Cook for 4 hours on low. Shred the chicken and toss with the prepared sauce.
- Serve with rice or cooked noodles.

Nutrients: Kcal: 347, Fats: 34 g, Total Carbs: 28 g, Proteins: 16 g.

15. Chicken & Gravy

Prep Time: 5 minutes

Cook Time: 5 hours

Servings: 2

Ingredients

- 1 cup of hot steamed rice
- ½ cup of chicken broth
- ¼ cup of chicken gravy mix
- 2 cups of cream chicken soup
- 3-4 boneless skinless chicken breasts

Instructions

- Add all ingredients to the crockpot.
- Cook for 4-5 hours on low.
- Slice the chicken before serving.

Nutrients: Kcal: 227, Fats: 32 g, Total Carbs: 26 g, Proteins: 19 g.

16. Meatball Stroganoff

Prep Time: 10 minutes

Cook Time: 6 hours

Servings: 4

Ingredients

- 1 small, sweet onion gluten-free
- 1 tbsp of minced garlic
- ½ cup of brown gravy gluten-free
- 1 cup of sour cream
- 1 tbsp of Worcestershire sauce
- 2 cups of cream of mushroom soup gluten-free
- 1 cup of beef broth
- 6 oz of rotini pasta gluten-free
- 4 oz of sliced mushrooms
- 12 oz of frozen meatballs, gluten-free

Instructions

- Put all ingredients in the crockpot except sour cream and noodles.
- Cook for 4-5 hours on low.
- Add sour cream and cook for 15 minutes.
- Add cooked pasta to the bowl, top with prepared meatballs and serve.

Nutrients: Kcal: 514, Fats: 21 g, Total Carbs: 24 g, Proteins: 15.6 g.

17. Parmesan Garlic Chicken & Potatoes

Prep Time: 10 minutes

Cook Time: 4 hours

Servings: 2

Ingredients

- 1 ½ cups of milk
- 12 oz of Parmesan garlic sauce
- 4 oz of shredded Parmesan cheese
- 8 oz of cream cheese
- 10 oz of Yukon Gold Potatoes
- 2-4 boneless skinless chicken breasts

Instructions

- Marinate the chicken with all combined ingredients except potatoes.
- Add the marinated chicken to the crockpot. Cook for 2 hours on low.
- Stir potatoes, cream cheese and parmesan cheese into the pot.
- Cook for 1-2 hours on low.
- Shred the chicken and toss it well in the sauce before serving.

Nutrients: Kcal: 347, Fats: 34 g, Total Carbs: 28 g, Proteins: 16 g.

18. Mango Chicken Curry

Prep Time: 10 minutes

Cook Time: 6 hours

Servings: 2

Ingredients

- 1 tbsp of oil
- 1 tbsp of brown sugar
- 1 tsp of ground turmeric
- 1 tsp of coriander
- 2 tsp of curry powder
- 1 tsp of chicken stock powder
- 1 tsp of lemon or lime juice
- 1 cup of coconut milk
- 2 cloves garlic, sliced
- 1 brown onion, sliced
- 2 carrots, peeled and sliced
- ½ cup of mango slices
- 1 cup of green beans
- 4 chicken thighs

Instructions

- Sauté all ingredients in the crockpot for 10 minutes, except chicken and beans.
- Cook for 4 hours on low.
- Stir in beans and cook for 30 minutes.
- Garnish with chopped coriander and a few drops of lemon juice.

Nutrients: Kcal: 559, Fats: 14 g, Total Carbs: 53 g, Proteins: 57 g.

19. Crockpot Chicken Carbonara

Prep Time: 10 minutes

Cook Time: 4 hours

Servings: 2

Ingredients

- 2 tbsp of butter
- ¼ cup of sweet peas
- 3 oz of cream cheese, onion and chive
- ¾ cup of cooked bacon
- 8 oz of mushrooms
- 2 chicken thighs

Instructions

- Combine cream cheese with butter in a container. Coat the butter mixture over the chicken.
- Transfer the chicken with mushrooms to the crockpot. Cook for 4 hours on low or 2 hours on high.
- Add peas and bacon to the crockpot and cook for 10-15 minutes on low.
- Serve with mashed potatoes or cooked rice.

Nutrients: Kcal: 519, Fats: 106 g, Total Carbs: 8 g, Proteins: 44 g.

20. Tuscan Chicken

Prep Time: 10 minutes

Cook Time: 3 hours

Servings: 2

Ingredients

- ½ tsp of salt
- ½ tsp of Italian seasoning
- 1 tbsp of cornstarch
- 2 tsp of minced garlic
- ⅓ cup of sundried tomatoes chopped
- ¼ tsp of paprika
- ½ cup of chopped fresh spinach
- ⅛ tsp of black pepper
- 1 cup of heavy cream
- ¼ cup of shredded Parmesan cheese
- 2 boneless skinless chicken breasts

Instructions

- Combine garlic with cream, cornstarch, salt and pepper in a bowl.
- Add all ingredients with chicken to the crockpot, except sauce.
- Cook for 3 hours on low or 2 hours on high.
- Stir in spinach and cook for 20 minutes.
- Serve with tortillas or burritos.

Nutrients: Kcal: 260, Fats: 27 g, Total Carbs: 9 g, Proteins: 29 g.

21. Easy Rice & Chicken Casserole

Prep Time: 10 minutes

Cook Time: 4 hours

Servings: 2

Ingredients

- 1 tsp of kosher salt
- ¼ tsp of black pepper
- 2 garlic cloves minced
- 1 cup of frozen peas
- 1 small yellow onion diced
- 2 medium carrots diced
- 1 ½ cups of white rice
- 3 cups of low-sodium stock
- 10 oz of condensed cream of mushroom soup
- 10 oz of raw chicken breasts diced

Instructions

- Add all ingredients to the crockpot except condensed soup and peas.
- Cook for 4-6 hours on low.
- Add peas and condensed soup to the pot and cook for 15 minutes on low.

Nutrients: Kcal: 347, Fats: 34 g, Total Carbs: 28 g, Proteins: 16 g.

22. Stuffed Asparagus Chicken Breasts

Prep Time: 5 minutes

Cook Time: 3 hours

Servings: 2

Ingredients

- 1 tbsp of Lawrey's salt
- 1 tsp of ground black pepper
- ⅔ cup of milk
- 1 cup of cream celery soup
- 1 cup of cream chicken soup
- 2 cups of shredded cheddar cheese
- 4 boneless skinless chicken breasts

Instructions

- Mix chicken breasts with salt and pepper. Mix well.
- Mix the cream soup with milk and shredded cheese in a separate bowl and toss to combine.
- Add the chicken breasts to the crockpot and spoon the prepared soup mixture over it.
- Layer the asparagus pieces on the chicken breast and season with salt and pepper.
- Cook for 4 hours on low.
- Drizzle some shredded cheese on top before serving.

Nutrients: Kcal: 506, Fats: 31 g, Total Carbs: 14 g, Proteins: 42 g.

23. Mongolian Chicken

Prep Time: 5 minutes

Cook Time: 4 hours

Servings: 2

Ingredients

- 1/2 cup of dark brown sugar
- ½ tsp of garlic powder
- 1/2 tsp of ground ginger
- 1 tsp of sesame seeds

- ¼ cup of low-sodium soy sauce
- 1 green onion, sliced
- 4 chicken thighs

Instructions

- Combine all the ingredients in a bowl.
- Transfer the chicken thighs to the crockpot and cover.
- Cook for 4 hours on low until chicken becomes tender.
- Season with sesame seeds and spring onions before serving.

Nutrients: Kcal: 339, Fats: 18 g, Total Carbs: 22 g, Proteins: 19 g.

24. Crockpot Chicken Breast

Prep Time: 10 minutes

Cook Time: 6 hours

Servings: 2

Ingredients

- ½ tsp of paprika
- ½ tsp of dried thyme
- 1 tsp of salt
- 1/2 tsp of onion powder
- 2 tbsp of olive oil
- ¼ tsp of pepper
- ½ cup of chicken broth
- 4 large chicken breasts
- ¼ tsp of garlic powder

Instructions

- Combine all the spices and seasonings in a bowl.
- Place the chicken breasts with olive oil in the bowl and rub well, so the sauces spread evenly.
- Transfer the marinated chicken with chicken broth into the crockpot.
- Cook for 3-4 hours on low. Serve with

desired toppings and tortillas.

Nutrients: Kcal: 324, Fats: 13 g, Total Carbs: 1 g, Proteins: 48 g.

25. Honey Garlic Chicken

Prep Time: 5 minutes

Cook Time: 4 hours

Servings: 2

Ingredients

- 1/3 cup of honey
- 1 tbsp of rice vinegar
- 2 tsp of chili paste, sriracha
- 2 tbsp of tomato paste
- 4 cloves of garlic minced
- 1/3 cup of low-sodium soy sauce
- 2 tbsp of cornstarch
- 1 cup of boneless, skinless chicken thighs

Instructions

- Combine all seasonings and spices in a bowl. Pour this mixture into the chicken and transfer to the crockpot.
- Cook for 4 hours on low. Change the sides of the chicken so that it can be cooked properly.
- Remove the chicken from the pot and add corn starch mixture; cook for 15 minutes until the sauce thickens.
- Shred the chicken on a separate plate. Stir in the shredded chicken to the pot.
- Serve with sesame seeds, onions and cooked rice.

Nutrients: Kcal: 329, Fats: 7 g, Total Carbs: 32 g, Proteins: 35 g.

26. Thai Peanut Chicken

Prep Time: 35 minutes

Cook Time: 4 hours

Servings: 2

Ingredients

- 2 tbsp of fresh lime juice
- 2 tbsp of coconut sugar
- ¼ tsp of crushed red pepper flakes
- 1 tbsp of minced garlic
- 2 tbsp of minced fresh ginger
- 1 tsp of fresh cilantro, chopped
- 2 tbsp of fish sauce
- 3 tbsp of red curry paste
- 1 small butternut squash
- ¼ cup of peanut butter creamy
- 2 cups of light coconut milk
- 1 medium yellow onion
- 2 large red bell peppers
- 2 cups of frozen peas thawed
- 1 cup of brown rice, cooked
- 10 oz of boneless skinless chicken breast

Instructions

- Add all spices to the crockpot. Cook until smoothens.
- Place chicken pieces with red pepper, onions and squash in the pot.
- Toss well and cook for 3-4 hours on low.
- Add peas and cook for 30 minutes.
- Squeeze lime juice before serving.
- Serve with cooked rice and chopped cilantro on top.

Nutrients: Kcal: 509, Fats: 19 g, Total Carbs: 40 g, Proteins: 42 g.

27. Santa Fe Chicken

Prep Time: 5 minutes

Cook Time: 6 hours

Servings: 2

Ingredients

- 1 tsp of salt
- 1 tsp of cayenne pepper
- 1 tsp of cumin
- 1 tsp of onion powder
- 1 tsp of garlic powder
- ¼ cup of chopped fresh cilantro
- 3 scallions, chopped
- 2 cups of chicken broth
- 8 oz of frozen corn
- 10 oz of chicken breast
- 1 cup of tomatoes with green chilies
- 1 cup of black beans, rinsed and drained

Instructions

- Mix chicken broth with all ingredients in a bowl, except chicken.
- Add chicken and prepared seasonings to the crockpot and season with salt.
- Cook for 3-4 hours on high.
- Shred the chicken on a plate. Stir the shredded chicken into the pot and toss well.
- Serve with desired toppings and cooked rice.

Nutrients: Kcal: 183, Fats: 3 g, Total Carbs: 17 g, Proteins: 24 g.

28. Honey Sesame Chicken

Prep Time: 15 minutes

Cook Time: 4 hours

Servings: 2

Ingredients

- ¼ cup of honey
- 1 tsp of sesame oil
- 1 tsp of black pepper
- 1 tsp of onion powder
- 2 cloves garlic, minced
- 1 tbsp of cornstarch
- 1/3 cup of low-sodium soy sauce
- 1 tsp of sriracha hot chili sauce
- ¼ cup of tomato paste
- 3 tbsp of rice wine vinegar
- ¼ cup of water
- ½ tbsp of sesame seeds
- 2 medium scallions, chopped
- 10 oz of boneless, skinless chicken breast

Instructions

- Season chicken with salt and pepper. Transfer the chicken to the crockpot.
- Mix all spices and seasonings in a bowl. Pour this mixture over the chicken.
- Cook for 3-4 hours on low. Shred the chicken on a plate.
- Add corn starch mixture, prepared with some water, to the crockpot. Cook for 20 minutes on high.
- Stir in chicken and toss well. Serve with cooked rice, scallions and sesame seeds.

Nutrients: Kcal: 198, Fats: 4 g, Total Carbs: 13.5 g, Proteins: 27 g.

29. Maple Dijon Chicken

Prep Time: 15 minutes

Cook Time: 2 hours

Servings: 2

Ingredients

- ¾ tsp of garlic salt
- 1 tsp of pepper
- ¼ cup of Dijon mustard
- 2 tbsp of balsamic vinegar
- ¼ cup of pure Maple syrup
- 4 skinless drumsticks

Instructions

- Rub chicken with garlic and seasonings. Place the chicken in the crockpot.
- Mix Dijon sauce with maple syrup and balsamic vinegar in a bowl. Mix well until all sauces blend well.
- Drizzle the sauce mixture over the drumsticks. Cook for 2 hours on low.

Nutrients: Kcal: 355, Fats: 9 g, Total Carbs: 18 g, Proteins: 48 g.

30. Herbed Chicken

Prep Time: 5 minutes

Cook Time: 2 hours

Servings: 2

Ingredients

- 1 tsp of paprika
- ½ tsp of dried basil
- ½ tsp of dried thyme
- ½ tsp of garlic powder
- ½ tsp of pepper
- ½ tsp of browning sauce
- 1 tbsp of olive oil
- ½ cup of chicken broth

- ½ tsp of seasoned salt
- 4 bone-in chicken breast

Instructions

- Add all ingredients to the crockpot.
- Rub chicken with browning sauce.
- Ladle broth to the crockpot, place the lid and cook for 2 hours on low.
- Serve with desired seasonings.

Nutrients: Kcal: 211, Fats: 7 g, Total Carbs: 1 g, Proteins: 33 g.

Chapter 12: Fish & Seafood Recipes

1. Seafood Chowder

Prep Time: 15 minutes

Cook Time: 3 hours 30 minutes

Servings: 2

Ingredients

- 1 tsp of salt
- ¼ tsp of crushed red pepper flakes
- ⅛ tsp of cayenne pepper
- 1 tsp of ground black pepper
- 1 tsp of dried oregano
- 1 tsp of dried basil
- ½ tsp of celery
- 1 tsp of dried thyme
- 1 tbsp of chopped fresh parsley
- 1 tbsp of tomato paste
- 3 clove garlic, minced
- ½ cup of chopped onion
- 1 cup of crushed tomatoes
- 1 cup of yellow potatoes
- 3 cups of vegetable broth
- 12 oz of seafood

Instructions

- Combine all ingredients in the crockpot except seafood.
- Cook for 3 hours on low or 2 hours on high.
- Add seafood to the crockpot and cook for 30 minutes on low.
- Add chopped parsley or cilantro on top before serving.

Nutrients: Kcal: 184, Fats: 2 g, Total Carbs: 18 g, Proteins: 26 g.

2. Italian Fish Chowder

Prep Time: 30 minutes

Cook Time: 4 hours

Servings: 2

Ingredients

- ½ tsp of red pepper flakes
- 1 tsp of ground black pepper
- 2 stalks of celery, diced
- 2 cloves garlic, minced
- 1 onion, chopped
- 2 potatoes, diced
- 2 carrots, diced
- 1 cup of fresh corn kernels
- 1 cup of evaporated milk
- 3 cups of chicken stock
- 4 slices of bacon, chopped
- 5 oz of halibut
- 1 cup of scallops
- 1 cup of uncooked shrimp

Instructions

- Sauté bacon in olive oil for 5-8 minutes until browned.
- Add onion and garlic to it and cook for 5 minutes.

- Transfer the bacon with all ingredients to the crockpot, except the seafood.
- Cook for 3 hours on high.
- Add seafood to the crockpot. Cook for 1 hour until thickens.

Nutrients: Kcal: 235, Fats: 6 g, Total Carbs: 28 g, Proteins: 18 g.

3. Fish Au Gratin

Prep Time: 15 minutes

Cook Time: 2 hours

Servings: 2

Ingredients

- 1 ½ tsp of salt
- ¼ tbsp of ground nutmeg
- 3 tbsp of flour
- ½ tbsp of dry mustard
- 6 tbsp of butter
- 1 ½ tsp of lemon juice
- 1 ¼ cup of milk
- 1 cup of cheddar cheese, shredded
- 10 oz of frozen white fish fillets

Instructions

- Grease the crockpot with butter.
- Add flour with nutmeg, salt and mustard to the crockpot. Cook for 3-4 minutes.
- Pour milk and cook until thickens. Add cheese with lemon juice and let it melt.
- Add fish to the pot and cook for 1 hour on high or 2 hours on low.
- Serve with some extra cheese on top.

Nutrients: Kcal: 347, Fats: 34 g, Total Carbs: 28 g, Proteins: 16 g.

4. Cioppino

Prep Time: 20 minutes

Cook Time: 4 hours

Servings: 2

Ingredients

- 1 tbsp of olive oil
- ½ tsp of sugar
- 1-2 tbsp of Italian seasoning
- 2 tbsp of minced fresh parsley
- 3 celery ribs, chopped
- 1 tbsp of red wine vinegar
- ½ cup of tomato paste
- ½ cup white wine
- 1 cup of clam juice
- 3 garlic cloves, minced
- 2 onions, chopped
- 1 cup of diced tomatoes
- 1 bay leaf
- 1 cup of lump crabmeat
- 1 cup of chopped clam
- 8 oz of uncooked shrimp
- 8 oz of haddock fillets

Instructions

- Mix all ingredients in the crockpot except seafood.
- Cook for 4 hours on low or 2 hours on high.
- Add seafood to the pot and cook for 30 minutes until tender.
- Top with chopped parsley before serving.

Nutrients: Kcal: 205, Fats: 3 g, Total Carbs: 15 g, Proteins: 29 g.

5. Seafood Boil

Prep Time: 20 minutes

Cook Time: 4 hours

Servings: 2

Ingredients

- ¼ cup of bay seasoning
- 4 tbsp of minced garlic
- 6 cups of water
- 1 lemon
- 8 oz of potatoes
- 2 ears of corn
- 10 oz of shrimp
- 10 oz of Cajun smoked Andouille

Instructions

- Layer potatoes with corn and sausages into the crockpot.
- Add water with bay seasonings, garlic and lemons on top.
- Cook for 4 hours on low or 2 hours on high.
- Stir in shrimp and cook for 15 minutes on low.
- Serve with cooked rice and melted butter.

Nutrients: Kcal: 372, Fats: 24 g, Total Carbs: 28 g, Proteins: 19 g.

6. Fish Pie

Prep Time: 20 minutes

Cook Time: 3 hours

Servings: 2

Ingredients

- 2 tbsp of butter
- 2 tbsp of plain flour
- 1 bay leaf
- ¼ cup of cheese
- 1 cup of milk
- ½ cup of fish stock
- 1 leek sliced
- 10 oz of mixed fish

Instructions

- Sauté leeks in a little olive oil. Put butter with flour and milk into the pan.
- Cook for 5-10 minutes and stir in cheese, stock and bay leaf.
- Add fish to the bottom of the crockpot. Spoon the sauce mixture over it.
- Cook for 2-3 hours on low.
- Serve with roasted tomatoes or mashed potatoes.

Nutrients: Kcal: 347, Fats: 34 g, Total Carbs: 28 g, Proteins: 16 g.

7. Crock Pot Shrimp Boil

Prep Time: 10 minutes

Cook Time: 4 hours

Servings: 2

Ingredients

- ¼ cup of butter
- 1 onion sliced
- 3 tbsp of minced garlic
- 5 oz of potatoes
- 2 bay leaves
- 2 tbsp of old bay
- 1 lemon
- 2 cups of vegetable broth
- 1 ½ cob of corn
- 5 oz of sausage, kielbasa
- 5 oz of shrimp

Instructions

- Add potatoes with onions, garlic, bay leaves and broth to the crockpot.

- Cook for 4 hours on low.
- Place the remaining ingredients into the pot and cook for 45 minutes on low.
- Discard the bay leaves before serving.

Nutrients: Kcal: 323, Fats: 28 g, Total Carbs: 12 g, Proteins: 6 g.

8. Creamy Salmon with Lemon Sauce

Prep Time: 10 minutes

Cook Time: 2 hours 30 minutes

Servings: 2

Ingredients

- 1 tsp of salt
- 1 tsp of ground pepper
- 1/2 tsp of chili powder
- ½ tsp of sweet paprika
- 1 tbsp of fresh parsley
- 1 tsp of Italian Seasoning
- 1 tsp of garlic powder
- 1/8 tsp of lemon zest
- ¼ cup of white wine
- 2 tbsp of lemon juice
- 2/3 cup of heavy cream
- 3 lemons
- 1 cup of low-sodium vegetable broth
- 10 oz of salmon fillet

Instructions

- Grease the crockpot with butter.
- Layer slices of lemon in the bottom of the pot. Add salmon on top and season with all spices.
- Ladle broth into the crockpot. Cook for 2 hours on low.
- Add cream with broth and lemon juice to the pan to prepare the sauce.

- Cook for 10 minutes.
- Drizzle the sauce over the salmon before serving.

Nutrients: Kcal: 330, Fats: 19 g, Total Carbs: 7 g, Proteins: 31 g.

9. Fish Curry

Prep Time: 15 minutes

Cook Time: 2 hours

Servings: 2

Ingredients

- 1 tsp of kosher salt
- 1 tsp of turmeric
- 1 tsp of ground cumin
- 1 tbsp of mild curry powder
- 2 tbsp of tamarind paste
- 1 tsp of whole coriander seeds
- 1 tbsp of cilantro
- ¼ tsp of fenugreek seeds
- ½ onion, chopped
- 2 cloves garlic, thinly sliced
- 1 tbsp of ginger, chopped
- 2 serrano chiles, sliced
- ½ cup of flaked unsweetened coconut
- 2 cups of unsweetened coconut milk
- 10 oz of firm white fish fillets

Instructions

- Blend ginger, coconut, turmeric, chiles, curry powder, coriander seeds, cumin, onion, fenugreek, garlic, tamarind, and salt in a blender. Blend well until puree.
- Add this mixture with coconut milk to the crockpot. Cook for 4 hours on low.
- Add salt and pepper to the fish and transfer to the crockpot.
- Cook for 20 minutes, until tender.

Nutrients: Kcal: 347, Fats: 34 g, Total Carbs: 28 g, Proteins: 16 g.

10. Seafood Bisque

Prep Time: 20 minutes

Cook Time: 3 hours

Servings: 2

Ingredients

- 2 tsp of kosher salt
- ¼ tsp of red pepper flakes
- 2 tsp of ground black pepper
- ¼ cup of all-purpose flour
- 2 tsp of old bay seasoning
- 3 tbsp of unsalted butter
- 3 cloves of garlic
- ⅓ cup of tomato paste
- 1 cup of diced tomatoes
- 1 cup of heavy whipping cream
- ¼ cup of dry white wine
- 4 cups of seafood stock
- 2 shallots
- 10 oz of Shrimp
- 8 oz of lump Crab meat

Instructions

- Grease the crockpot with butter.
- Add shallots with garlic to the pot. Cook for 10 minutes.
- Add diced tomatoes with seasonings and stock to the crockpot.
- Combine whipping cream with white wine and all-purpose flour in a bowl. Spoon this mixture into the crockpot.
- Cook for 4 hours on low or 2 hours on high.
- Add lump crab meat and shrimp to the pot.

- Cook for 30 minutes on high or 45 minutes on low.

Nutrients: Kcal: 334, Fats: 19 g, Total Carbs: 19 g, Proteins: 22 g.

11. Seafood Paella

Prep Time: 10 minutes

Cook Time: 4 hours

Servings: 2

Ingredients

- 1 ½ cups of jasmine rice
- ½ cup of water
- 2 cups of vegetable broth
- 2 tsp of salt
- 2 tsp of pepper
- 2 tsp of smoked paprika
- 1 tsp of garlic powder
- ½ tsp of red pepper flakes
- 4 Spanish chorizo links, sliced
- 1-2 tbsp of cilantro
- ½ tbsp of lemon juice
- 1 cup of chopped tomatoes
- ½ cup of frozen peas
- 5 oz of shrimp
- 3 scallions chopped
- 10 scallops

Instructions

- Add all ingredients to the crockpot except seafood and peas.
- Cook for 4 hours on low.
- Add peas with scallops and shrimp to the crockpot. Season with salt and pepper.
- Cook for 30 minutes on low.
- Top with chopped cilantro before serving.

Nutrients: Kcal: 328, Fats: 12.5 g, Total Carbs: 35 g, Proteins: 19 g.

12. Fish Fillets

Prep Time: 20 minutes

Cook Time: 3 hours

Servings: 2

Ingredients

- 1 tsp of salt
- 1 tsp of pepper
- 2-3 lemons
- 2-3 bay leaves
- 10 oz of fish fillets

Instructions

- Season fillets with white wine, lemon slices and bay leaves.
- Wrap fillets in aluminum foil. Place the fillets in the crockpot.
- Cook for 1 hour on high or 3 hours on low until done.

Nutrients: Kcal: 297, Fats: 21 g, Total Carbs: 29 g, Proteins: 16 g.

13. Lemon Dill Halibut

Prep Time: 5 minutes

Cook Time: 1 hour 30 minutes

Servings: 2

Ingredients

- 1 tbsp of olive oil
- 1 tbsp of lemon juice
- 1 tsp of salt
- 1 tsp of pepper
- 1 ½ tsp of dried dill
- 12 oz of wild halibut

Instructions

- Mix dill, olive oil and lemon juice in a container.

- Season halibut with salt and pepper. Add halibut to the crockpot.
- Ladle the dill mixture over the halibut. Cook for 2 hours on high.
- Top with chopped cilantro and a few drops of lemon juice.
- Serve with cooked rice or roasted tomatoes.

Nutrients: Kcal: 347, Fats: 34 g, Total Carbs: 28 g, Proteins: 16 g.

14. Shrimp Creole

Prep Time: 15 minutes

Cook Time: 4 hours

Servings: 2

Ingredients

- 2 tsp of sugar
- 1 tsp of salt
- 1 tsp of red pepper flakes, crushed
- ½ tsp of ground black pepper
- 1 tsp of tabasco
- ¾ cup of chopped celery
- 1 bay leaf
- 2 cups of tomato puree
- 1 ½ onion chopped
- 2 tbsp of garlic, minced
- 1 green bell pepper, chopped
- 10 oz of shrimp

Instructions

- Add all ingredients to the crockpot except shrimp.
- Cook for 4 hours on low or 2 hours on high.
- Add shrimp to the crockpot and cook for 15 minutes. Serve with cooked rice.

Nutrients: Kcal: 265, Fats: 2 g, Total Carbs: 28 g, Proteins: 32 g.

15. Tilapia with Lemon

Prep Time: 10 minutes

Cook Time: 2 hours

Servings: 2

Ingredients

- ½ tsp of salt
- 1 tsp of pepper
- 2 tbsp of unsalted butter
- 1 lemon
- 4 tilapia fillets

Instructions

- Grease the crockpot with butter.
- Layer tilapia with lemon on top, in the bottom of the crockpot.
- Cook for 2 hours on low.
- Serve with chopped cilantro on top.

Nutrients: Kcal: 349, Fats: 19 g, Total Carbs: 24 g, Proteins: 76 g.

16. Bouillabaisse

Prep Time: 30 minutes

Cook Time: 3 hours

Servings: 2

Ingredients

- 2 tbsp of olive oil
- ¼ tsp of coarse sea salt
- ¼ tsp of ground black pepper
- ¼ tsp of cayenne pepper
- 1 cup of sliced celery
- ¼ tsp of saffron threads
- ½ tsp of shredded lemon peel
- 3 cloves garlic, minced
- 1 cup of chopped onion
- 1 cup of roasted tomatoes
- 5 oz of potatoes
- 1 cup of baby carrots
- 1 fennel bulb
- 1 ½ cups of firm-textured bread
- 2 cups of vegetable broth
- 1 cup of cracked black pepper Croutons
- 8 oz of frozen skinless cod
- 10 oz of frozen shrimp in shells

Instructions

- Add all veggies and spices to the crockpot, except seafood. Cook for 2 hours on low.
- Add saffron to the scallops, shrimp and fish. Cook for 30 minutes on low.
- Combine cooked seafood with the prepared mixture and serve with black pepper croutons.

Nutrients: Kcal: 344, Fats: 7 g, Total Carbs: 42 g, Proteins: 28 g.

Chapter 13: Desserts

1. Rice Pudding

Prep Time: 10 minutes

Cook Time: 4 hours

Servings: 2

Ingredients

- ¼ tsp of salt
- 2 tbsp of brown sugar
- ½ tsp of cinnamon
- 1 tbsp of butter
- ⅓ tsp of vanilla extract
- 2 cups of whole milk
- ¾ cup of sugar
- 1 cup of white rice, uncooked

Instructions

- Add all ingredients to greased crockpot.
- Add some butter on top.
- Cook for 4 hours on low.
- Season with cinnamon before serving.

Nutrients: Kcal: 316, Fats: 10 g, Total Carbs: 48 g, Proteins: 7 g.

2. Lemon Curd Cake

Prep Time: 5 minutes

Cook Time: 2 hours

Servings: 2

Ingredients

- 1/3 cup of vegetable oil
- 1 cup of water
- 3 eggs
- 1-2 tbsp of powdered sugar
- ½ cup of lemon curd
- 1-2 cups of Lemon Supreme cake mix

Instructions

- Blend eggs with vegetable oil and water.
- Add this mixture to the crockpot.
- Microwave lemon curd for 30 seconds and stir in the crockpot.
- Cook for 2 hours on low.
- Drizzle some powdered sugar over it and serve with vanilla ice cream.

Nutrients: Kcal: 209, Fats: 12 g, Total Carbs: 38 g, Proteins: 2 g.

3. Apple Butter

Prep Time: 30 minutes

Cook Time: 6 hours

Servings: 2

Ingredients

- ¼ tsp of ground cloves
- ¼ tsp of salt
- ½ tsp of freshly grated nutmeg
- 1 cup of brown sugar
- 1 cup of granulated sugar
- 1 tbsp of ground cinnamon
- 1 tbsp of pure vanilla extract

- 4 apples

Instructions

- Mix sugar with salt, nutmeg and cinnamon in a bowl.
- Layer apples in the bottom of the crockpot and spoon the prepared mixture over it.
- Cook for 4 hours on low.
- Add vanilla on top and cook for 2 hours.
- Add this mixture to the blender and blend well until puree.
- Serve with bread or tortillas.

Nutrients: Kcal: 40, Fats: 0 g, Total Carbs: 30 g, Proteins: 0 g.

4. Four Ingredient Christmas Cake

Prep Time: 15 minutes

Cook Time: 4 hours

Servings: 2

Ingredients

- 2 cups of flour
- ½-¾ cup of Baileys
- 2 cups of chocolate milk
- 1-2 cups of mixed fruit

Instructions

- Add Baileys with mixed fruit in a bowl.
- Stir in flour and scoop into the crockpot.
- Cover and cook for 4 hours, until browned.

Nutrients: Kcal: 37, Fats: 4 g, Total Carbs: 7.8 g, Proteins: 5.6 g.

5. Potato Gem Pie

Prep Time: 20 minutes

Cook Time: 2 hours

Servings: 2

Ingredients

- 1 tsp of salt
- 1 tsp of pepper
- 1 tsp of minced garlic
- ½ cup of flour
- ¼ cup of Worcestershire sauce
- 1 cup of beef stock
- 1 onion grated
- 1 stalk of celery grated
- 2 carrots grated
- 1 egg
- ½ cup of grated cheese
- 1 cup of potato gems
- 3-4 sheets of puff pastry

Instructions

- Combine all dry ingredients in a bowl.
- Layer sheets of pastry with eggs in the crockpot.
- Add the prepared mixture and potato gems on top.
- Drizzle some shredded cheese.
- Cook for 2 hours on high.

Nutrients: Kcal: 347, Fats: 34 g, Total Carbs: 28 g, Proteins: 16 g.

6. Apple Cobbler

Prep Time: 10 minutes

Cook Time: 4 hours 5 minutes

Servings: 1

Ingredients

- 1 tbsp of cinnamon sugar
- 1 tbsp of vanilla ice cream
- 3 tbsp of unsalted butter, melted
- ½ tsp of cinnamon
- 1 cup of white cake mix
- 2 cups of apple pie fillings

Instructions

- Mix all dry ingredients in a bowl.
- Combine apples with pie filling and cinnamon sugar.
- Grease the crockpot with melted butter.
- Scoop the pie mixture at the bottom of the crockpot. Add dry mixture over it.
- Cook for 4 hours on low or 2 hours on high.
- Serve with vanilla ice cream.

Nutrients: Kcal: 571, Fats: 14 g, Total Carbs: 110 g, Proteins: 3 g.

7. Cinnamon Apples

Prep Time: 10 minutes

Cook Time: 3 hours

Servings: 1

Ingredients

- 2 tsp of cinnamon
- 2 tbsp of butter
- 2/3 cup of granulated sugar
- 6 apples

Instructions

- Mix apples with sugar and cinnamon.
- Grease the crockpot with butter.
- Scoop the apple mixture into the pot.
- Cook for 3 hours on high.
- Sprinkle some cinnamon and serve.

Nutrients: Kcal: 215, Fats: 4 g, Total Carbs: 47 g, Proteins: 1 g.

8. Chocolate Cherry Cobbler

Prep Time: 5 minutes

Cook Time: 4 hours

Servings: 2

Ingredients

- 6 tbsp of melted butter
- 6 tbsp of vanilla ice cream
- 1 cup of chocolate cake mix
- 1 cup of cherry pie fillings
- ½ cup of Maraschino cherries

Instructions

- Layer cherry pie filling in the bottom of the crockpot.
- Stir in the dry cake mix with some melted butter over it.
- Cook for 4 hours on low or 2 hours on high.

Nutrients: Kcal: 780, Fats: 30 g, Total Carbs: 128 g, Proteins: 7 g.

9. Crockpot Hot Chocolate

Prep Time: 5 minutes

Cook Time: 2 hours

Servings: 2

Ingredients

- ½ cup of milk chocolate chips
- 1 cup of heavy cream
- ½ cup of dark chocolate chips
- 3-4 tbsp of chocolate shavings
- ¼ cup of marshmallows

- 1-2 tbsp of whipped cream
- ½ cup of white chocolate chips
- ½ cup of sweetened condensed milk
- 4 cups of milk

Instructions

- Combine all ingredients in the crockpot except marshmallows.
- Toss well to combine.
- Cook for 2-3 hours on low, stirring continuously.
- Stir in marshmallows and cook for 30 minutes.

Nutrients: Kcal: 521, Fats: 31 g, Total Carbs: 50 g, Proteins: 10 g.

10. Baked Apple Crisp

Prep Time: 10 minutes

Cook Time: 1 hour 15 minutes

Servings: 1

Ingredients

- ¼ tsp of sea salt
- ½ cup of brown sugar
- ½ cup of flour
- 2 tbsp of lemon juice
- 1/3 cup of unsalted butter
- ½ cup of rolled oats whole, uncooked
- ¼ tsp of cinnamon
- 4 cups of sweet apples

Instructions

- Grease the crockpot with some butter.
- Mix all ingredients except apples and lemon juice. Blend well until puree.
- Layer apples with lemon juice in the greased crockpot.
- Scoop the prepared mixture over it.
- Cook for 1 hour on low or 45 minutes

on high.

Nutrients: Kcal: 251, Fats: 9 g, Total Carbs: 42 g, Proteins: 2 g.

11. Chocolate Caramel Cake

Prep Time: 15 minutes

Cook Time: 2 hours

Servings: 2

Ingredients

- 3 eggs
- 1 ¼ cup of water
- 3/4 cup of vegetable oil
- 1 tbsp of vanilla extract
- ½ cup of caramel sauce
- ¼ cup of cool whip
- 1/2 cup of chopped health bars
- 1 cup of chocolate chips
- 1 cup of sweetened condensed milk
- 1 cup of Chocolate cake mix

Instructions

- Combine all ingredients in the crockpot.
- Grease the crockpot with butter. Pour this mixture into the crockpot.
- Sprinkle extra chocolate chips on top. Cook for 2 hours.
- Drizzle half a cup of condensed milk on top and cook for 30 minutes on low until done.

Nutrients: Kcal: 485, Fats: 25 g, Total Carbs: 61 g, Proteins: 6 g.

12. Reese's Peanut Butter Cupcakes

Prep Time: 15 minutes

Cook Time: 2 hours

Servings: 2

Ingredients

- 3 eggs
- 1 cup of water
- 2 tbsp of powdered sugar
- 10 peanut butter cups
- 1 cup of creamy peanut butter
- ½ cup of salted butter, melted
- 2 cups of devil's food cake mix

Instructions

- Grease the crockpot with butter.
- Combine all ingredients in a bowl. Add this mixture to the peanut butter cups.
- Place these cups in the crockpot.
- Cook for 2 hours on high.
- Add peanut butter and sugar to the saucepan. Let it cook for 5 minutes.
- Add the prepared mixture to the peanut butter cups before serving.

Nutrients: Kcal: 607, Fats: 39 g, Total Carbs: 57 g, Proteins: 13 g.

13. Brownie Pudding

Prep Time: 15 minutes

Cook Time: 2 hours

Servings: 2

Ingredients

- 2 large eggs
- 2 cups of milk
- 3 tbsp of water
- ½ cup of vegetable oil
- 1 cup of chocolate fudge pudding mix
- 1 cup of Brownie Mix

Instructions

- Grease the crockpot with butter or vegetable oil.
- Combine all ingredients in a bowl. Whisk well to combine.
- Scoop this mixture into the crockpot.
- Cook for 2-3 hours on high.
- Serve with vanilla ice cream.

Nutrients: Kcal: 267, Fats: 32 g, Total Carbs: 19 g, Proteins: 14 g.

14. Rocky Road Cake

Prep Time: 20 minutes

Cook Time: 3 hours

Servings: 2

Ingredients

- 3 eggs
- 1/3 cup of melted butter
- 3 ¼ cups of milk
- 1 tsp of vanilla extract
- 1 cup of sour cream
- ½ cup of chopped pecans
- 1 cup of mini chocolate chips
- 1 ½ cups of miniature marshmallows
- 1 cup of chocolate cook-and-serve pudding mix
- 1 cup of chocolate instant pudding mix
- 1 cup of chocolate cake mix

Instructions

- Add all ingredients in the blender except milk and pecans. Blend well until batter forms.
- Grease the crockpot with butter. Scoop this mixture into the crockpot.
- Boil the milk in a separate container. Stir in the hot milk over the prepared

mixture.

- Cook for 3 hours on low.
- Sauté pecans in a pan for 5 minutes on low.
- Stir in pecans with marshmallows before serving.

Nutrients: Kcal: 198, Fats: 26 g, Total Carbs: 17 g, Proteins: 32 g.

15. Cherry Dump Cake

Prep Time: 10 minutes

Cook Time: 2 hours

Servings: 2

Ingredients

- ½ cup of unsalted butter
- 1 cup of yellow cake mix
- 1 ½ cups of cherry pie filling

Instructions

- Mix melted butter with all ingredients except cherry pie fillings and cake mix. Toss well to combine.
- Layer the cherry pie fillings at the bottom of the crockpot. Scoop the prepared mixture over it.
- Add dump cake mix with butter on top.
- Cook for 4 hours on low.

Nutrients: Kcal: 344, Fats: 9 g, Total Carbs: 63 g, Proteins: 1 g.

16. Smores Chocolate Cake

Prep Time: 15 minutes

Cook Time: 2 hours

Servings: 1

Ingredients

- ¼ cup of melted butter
- 1/3 cup of granulated sugar
- 2 cups of graham cracker crumbs
- 2 cups of mini marshmallows

- 1 cup of chocolate cake mix
- 2 cups of semi-sweet chocolate chips

Instructions

- Mix cake mix with half of the chocolate chips.
- Add the remaining ingredients to the crockpot, half of the chocolate chips and marshmallows.
- Ladle this chocolate chip mixture over it.
- Cook for 2 hours on low.
- Stir in the remaining chocolate chips and

Nutrients: Kcal: 472, Fats: 25 g, Total Carbs: 58 g, Proteins: 5 g.

17. Chocolate Lava Cake

Prep Time: 20 minutes

Cook Time: 3 hours

Servings: 2

Ingredients

- 3 eggs
- 2 cups of milk
- ½ cup of vegetable oil
- 1 cup of instant chocolate pudding
- 2 cups of milk chocolate chips
- 1 cup of triple chocolate fudge cake mix

Instructions

- Add all ingredients in a blender except milk. Blend well until smooth batter forms.
- Add this batter to the crockpot.
- Boil the milk and pour it over the batter.
- Cook for 3 hours on low until the cake is done.

Nutrients: Kcal: 670, Fats: 33 g, Total Carbs: 83 g, Proteins: 11 g.

18. Apple Dump Cake

Prep Time: 10 minutes

Cook Time: 4 hours

Servings: 1

Ingredients

- ¼ cup of granulated sugar
- 1 ½ tsp of cinnamon
- ½ cup of quick-cooking oats
- 1 cup of yellow cake mix
- ½ cup of butter, sliced
- 4 apples

Instructions

- Mix apples with cinnamon and sugar in the crockpot.
- Mix the remaining ingredients in a bowl and mix well.
- Stir in the prepared mixture and cover.
- Cook for 4 hours on low or 2 hours on high.
- Top with whipped cream before serving.

Nutrients: Kcal: 83, Fats: 1 g, Total Carbs: 21 g, Proteins: 1 g.

19. Chocolate Peanut Butter

Prep Time: 15 minutes

Cook Time: 1 hour 45 minutes

Servings: 2

Ingredients

- 3 eggs
- 1/4 cup of milk
- 1 cup of water
- 1 cup of powdered sugar
- 1/3 cup of butter, softened
- 1/4 cup of fudge sauce
- ½ cup of creamy peanut butter
- 12 miniature peanut butter cups
- 1 cup of chocolate cake mix

Instructions

- Grease the crockpot with butter or vegetable oil.
- Add all ingredients to the food processor and blend well.
- Spoon this batter into the greased crockpot.
- Cook for 1-2 hours on low or 45 minutes on high.
- Combine some extra peanut butter with sugar and milk to make a glaze.
- Pour this fudge on top of the cake before serving.

Nutrients: Kcal: 194, Fats: 29 g, Total Carbs: 21 g, Proteins: 19 g.

20. Chocolate Fondant Dessert

Prep Time: 5 minutes

Cook Time: 3 hours 15 minutes

Servings: 2

Ingredients

- 3 eggs
- 3 tbsp of icing sugar
- 1 cup of caster sugar
- 2 tbsp of plain flour
- 2-3 tbsp of cocoa powder

- ¼ cup of unsalted butter, chopped
- ½ cup of dark chocolate, chopped

Instructions

- Place the foil paper at the bottom of the crockpot.
- Add butter to the chocolate and let it melt for 5 minutes on low.
- Add flour with eggs, cocoa powder and sugar to the melted chocolate. Mix well until combined.
- Scoop this mixture into the crockpot, cover and cook for 2-3 hours on low.

Nutrients: Kcal: 298, Fats: 37 g, Total Carbs: 38 g, Proteins: 22 g.

21. Caramel Butterscotch Cake

Prep Time: 10 minutes

Cook Time: 2 hours

Servings: 2

Ingredients

- 2 tbsp of butter
- ½ cup of milk
- 1 ¾ cup of boiling water
- ¼ cup of caramel sauce
- 1 cup of butterscotch chips
- 1 cup of caramel cake mix

Instructions

- Grease the crockpot with butter or vegetable oil.
- Mix half of the cake mixture with melted butter.
- Mix the remaining cake mix with milk and whisk. Scoop this mixture into the crockpot.
- Layer the butterscotch chips at the bottom of the crockpot.
- Add the remaining mixture over it. Cook for 2 hours on low.

- Serve with extra caramel sauce or vanilla ice cream.

Nutrients: Kcal: 349, Fats: 17 g, Total Carbs: 49 g, Proteins: 2 g.

22. Caramel Apple Dump Cake

Prep Time: 10 minutes

Cook Time: 5 hours

Servings: 2

Ingredients

- 1/2 cup of unsalted butter cubed
- ½ cup of caramel ice cream
- ½ cup of chopped pecans
- 1 cup of box spice cake mix
- 1 cup of apple pie filling

Instructions

- Add apple pie filling to the greased crockpot.
- Add remaining ingredients on top. Season some butter over it.
- Cook for 4 hours on low or 2 hours on high.
- Serve with caramel sauce or vanilla ice cream.

Nutrients: Kcal: 217, Fats: 24 g, Total Carbs: 23 g, Proteins: 3 g.

23. Bread Pudding

Prep Time: 10 minutes

Cook Time: 3 hours

Servings: 2

Ingredients

- 2 eggs
- ¼ cup of white sugar
- ½ tsp of vanilla extract
- 2 cups of milk
- ¼ cup of butter, melted

- 1 cup of raisins
- ¼ tsp of ground nutmeg
- 2 cups of cubed bread

Instructions

- Combine all ingredients in the bowl except bread and raisins. Toss well.
- Put the bread and raisins in the bottom of the crockpot. Scoop the mixture over it.
- Cook for 3 hours on low.

Nutrients: Kcal: 397, Fats: 14 g, Total Carbs: 58 g, Proteins: 11 g.

24. Reindeer Poop

Prep Time: 10 minutes

Cook Time: 1 hour 30 minutes

Servings: 2

Ingredients

- 2 cups of dry-roasted peanuts
- 1 cup of semi-sweet chocolate chips
- 1 cup of sweet German chocolate, chopped
- 1 cup of white candy coating, coarsely chopped

Instructions

- Add all ingredients to the crockpot.
- Cook for 1 ½ hours on low.
- Toss well and cook for 10 minutes.
- Serve with some shredded chocolate on top.

Nutrients: Kcal: 174, Fats: 13 g, Total Carbs: 14 g, Proteins: 4 g.

25. Tapioca Pudding

Prep Time: 5 minutes

Cook Time: 3 hours

Servings: 2

Ingredients

- 2 eggs
- ⅔ cup of white sugar
- 4 cups of milk
- ½ cup of pearl tapioca

Instructions

- Add all ingredients to the crockpot.
- Cook for 3 hours on low.
- Add some cinnamon or icing sugar before serving.

Nutrients: Kcal: 191, Fats: 5 g, Total Carbs: 30 g, Proteins: 7 g.

26. Warm Berry Compote

Prep Time: 15 minutes

Cook Time: 1 hour 30 minutes

Servings: 2

Ingredients

- ½ cup of white sugar
- 2 tbsp of cornstarch
- 2 tbsp of water
- ¼ cup of orange juice
- 1 ½ tsp of grated orange zest
- 6 cups of frozen mixed berries

Instructions

- Mix all ingredients in the crockpot except the cornstarch mixture.
- Cook for 1-½ hours on low.
- Pour the cornstarch mixture into the crockpot.
- Cook for 15 minutes on low.

- Sprinkle some icing sugar before serving.

Nutrients: Kcal: 141, Fats: 1 g, Total Carbs: 37 g, Proteins: 1 g.

27. Fruit Cobbler

Prep Time: 10 minutes

Cook Time: 3 hours

Servings: 2

Ingredients

- ½ cup of brown sugar
- ½ tsp of ground cinnamon
- 2 tbsp of cornstarch
- 1 tsp of vanilla extract
- ½ cup of melted butter
- 2 cups of mixed frozen berries
- 1 cup of white cake mix
- ½ tsp of nutmeg
- 2 cups of frozen peach slices

Instructions

- Grease the crockpot with some butter.
- Mix all ingredients in a bowl except peaches and berries.
- Layer peaches and berries at the bottom of the crockpot.
- Scoop the mixture over it and toss well. Add some butter on top.
- Cook for 3 hours on low.

Nutrients: Kcal: 511, Fats: 19 g, Total Carbs: 88 g, Proteins: 14 g.

28. Apple Cinnamon Bread Pudding

Prep Time: 15 minutes

Cook Time: 3 hours

Servings: 2

Ingredients

- ½ cup of brown sugar

- 1-2 tbsp of cinnamon
- 1 tbsp of nutmeg
- 2 eggs
- 4 slices of bread
- 3-4 apples

Instructions

- Mix all ingredients in a bowl except bread and apples.
- Layer apples with bread in the bottom of the crockpot.
- Pour the prepared mixture over it.
- Cook for 3-4 hours on low.
- Sprinkle some ground cinnamon before serving.

Nutrients: Kcal: 26, Fats: 3 g, Total Carbs: 48 g, Proteins: 11 g.

29. Vanilla Tapioca Pudding

Prep Time: 5 minutes

Cook Time: 6 hours

Servings: 2

Ingredients

- 4 eggs
- 1 ⅓ cups of white sugar
- 1 tsp of vanilla extract
- 3-4 cups of whole milk
- 1 cup of pearl tapioca

Instructions

- Mix all ingredients in the crockpot.
- Cook for 6 hours on low.
- Add vanilla on top and serve.

Nutrients: Kcal: 218, Fats: 6 g, Total Carbs: 35 g, Proteins: 6 g.

30. Bananas Foster

Prep Time: 10 minutes

Cook Time: 2 hours

Servings: 2

Ingredients

- 1 cup of brown sugar
- ¼ cup of chopped walnuts
- ½ tsp of ground cinnamon
- 2 tbsp of butter, melted
- 1 tsp of vanilla extract
- ¼ cup of rum
- ¼ cup of shredded coconut
- 4 bananas, sliced

Instructions

- Mix all ingredients in a bowl except bananas.
- Place the slices of bananas in the bottom of the crockpot.
- Scoop the prepared mixture on top.
- Cook for 2 hours on low.
- Spoon some chopped walnuts and shredded coconut on top before serving.

Nutrients: Kcal: 539, Fats: 21 g, Total Carbs: 84 g, Proteins: 3 g.

Chapter 14: Snacks

1. Cheesy Potatoes

Prep Time: 5 minutes

Cook Time: 4 hours

Servings: 2

Ingredients

- 1 cup of French-fried onions
- 2 cups of condensed cheddar cheese soup
- 1 cup of evaporated milk
- 5 oz of hash brown potatoes

Instructions

- Combine all the ingredients in a container.
- Add some butter to the crockpot. Spoon all combined ingredients into the crockpot.
- Cook for 4 hours on high.
- Add fried onions on top and serve.

Nutrients: Kcal: 308, Fats: 15 g, Total Carbs: 37 g, Proteins: 9 g.

2. Steak Bites

Prep Time: 10 minutes

Cook Time: 6 hours

Servings: 2

Ingredients

- 4 tbsp of butter
- 1 tsp of salt
- 1 tsp of pepper
- 2 tsp of minced garlic
- ½ onion diced
- 1 cup of beef broth
- 12 oz of round steak

Instructions

- Combine all the ingredients in the container.
- Toss well and transfer to the crockpot.
- Cook for 6 hours on low.
- Serve with desired seasonings.

Nutrients: Kcal: 392, Fats: 18 g, Total Carbs: 1 g, Proteins: 52 g.

3. Cracker Barrel Hash Brown Casserole

Prep Time: 10 minutes

Cook Time: 2 hours

Servings: 2

Ingredients

- 1 tsp of salt
- 1 tsp of pepper
- 1 onion chopped
- ½ cup of melted butter
- ½ cup of cheddar cheese shredded
- 1 ½ cups Colby Jack cheese shredded
- 1 ½ cups of sour cream
- 10 oz of cream of chicken soup

- 10 oz of frozen hash browns

Instructions

- Grease the crockpot with some butter.
- Mix all ingredients with hashbrowns in a container and transfer to the crockpot.
- Season with salt and pepper.
- Cook for 4 hours on low or 2 hours on high.

Nutrients: Kcal: 318, Fats: 43.7 g, Total Carbs: 41.9 g, Proteins: 16 g.

4. Creamed Chipped Beef on Toast

Prep Time: 10 minutes

Cook Time: 1 hour

Servings: 2

Ingredients

- 1 tsp of cayenne pepper
- 2 tbsp of all-purpose flour
- 1 ½ cups of warm milk
- 2 tbsp of butter
- 4-6 slices of bread
- 1 cup of jar dried beef, chopped

Instructions

- Grease the crockpot with some butter.
- Add flour with milk to the crockpot and stir.
- Cook for 15 minutes on low, stirring continuously to avoid lumps.
- Add beef with cayenne to the pot and cook for 45 minutes on low.

Nutrients: Kcal: 197, Fats: 9 g, Total Carbs: 9 g, Proteins: 21 g.

5. Fried Potatoes with Onions

Prep Time: 10 minutes

Cook Time: 2 hours

Servings: 2

Ingredients

- ¼ tsp of salt
- ¼ tsp of pepper
- ½ tsp of dried oregano
- ¼ tsp of dried parsley
- ¼ tsp of dried thyme
- ¼ cup of melted butter
- ½ cup of extra virgin olive oil
- 1 oz of onion soup mix
- 10 oz of potatoes

Instructions

- Add sliced potatoes with ingredients to the crockpot.
- Mix well and cook for 2 hours on high.
- Serve with toast and top with extra fried onions.

Nutrients: Kcal: 497, Fats: 39 g, Total Carbs: 33 g, Proteins: 7 g.

6. Crockpot Tasty Ziti

Prep Time: 20 minutes

Cook Time: 2 hours 30 minutes

Servings: 2

Ingredients

- ⅓ cup of freshly chopped basil
- 1 cup of shredded mozzarella cheese
- 2 cups of freshly grated parmesan cheese
- 5 oz of ricotta cheese
- 2 eggs
- 12 oz of tomato sauce

- 5 oz of penne pasta
- 2 cups of pasta sauce

Instructions

- Add penne pasta with tomato and pasta sauce to the crockpot.
- Mix all remaining ingredients and transfer to the crockpot.
- Cook for 1 hour on high or 3 hours on low. Add parmesan cheese and mozzarella cheese on top and allow it to melt.
- Season with some pepper and chili flakes.

Nutrients: Kcal: 274, Fats: 13 g, Total Carbs: 28 g, Proteins: 26 g.

7. Chicken Lettuce Cups

Prep Time: 20 minutes

Cook Time: 5 hours 30 minutes

Servings: 2

Ingredients

- 1 tsp of kosher salt
- 1/8 tsp of red pepper
- 1 tsp of black pepper
- 2/3 cup of mayonnaise
- 1/3 cup of apple cider vinegar
- 4 garlic cloves, minced
- 1 apple
- 1 onion
- 6-8 Bibb lettuce leaves
- 4 uncooked bacon slices, chopped
- 4 oz of whole chicken

Instructions

- Add all ingredients to the crockpot except spices and red pepper.
- Cook for 3-4 hours on low. Shred the chicken on a plate.

- Put all liquid in a separate container and discard the remaining ingredients.
- Combine all spices with mayonnaise and reserved liquid.
- Add prepared chicken with some toppings and serve.

Nutrients: Kcal: 234, Fats: 19 g, Total Carbs: 21 g, Proteins: 16 g.

8. Cheddar Corn

Prep Time: 5 minutes

Cook Time: 3 hours

Servings: 2

Ingredients

- ½ tsp of salt
- ¼ tsp of pepper
- ¼ cup of butter
- 1 cup of shredded cheddar cheese
- ¼ cup of heavy cream
- 1 cup of cream cheese
- 10 oz of frozen corn

Instructions

- Add all ingredients to the crockpot.
- Cook for 3-4 hours on low.
- Add cheese on top before serving and toss well.

Nutrients: Kcal: 347, Fats: 34 g, Total Carbs: 28 g, Proteins: 16 g.

9. Five Cheese Macaroni

Prep Time: 15 minutes

Cook Time: 3 hours

Servings: 2

Ingredients

- 1½ tsp of salt
- 1½ tsp of smoked paprika
- 1½ tsp of garlic powder

- 1½ tsp of black pepper
- 2 tsp of all-purpose seasoning
- ¼ cup of diced onions
- 2 cups of half & half
- 2 ½ cups of whole milk
- ½ cup of melted butter
- 1 cup of cheddar cheese, grated
- ½ cup of Monterey jack cheese, grated
- 1 cup of mozzarella cheese, grated
- 1 cup of Colby jack cheese, grated
- ¼ cup of cream cheese
- 8 oz of elbow macaroni

Instructions

- Combine all seasonings with milk, cream cheese, onions and half & half.
- Boil macaroni in hot water. Stir in the milk mixture to the crockpot with macaroni and all five pieces of cheese.
- Cook for 3 hours on low or 1 ½ hours on high.
- Top with some extra cheddar cheese and pepper before serving.

Nutrients: Kcal: 347, Fats: 34 g, Total Carbs: 28 g, Proteins: 16 g.

10. Grape Jelly Meatballs

Prep Time: 10 minutes

Cook Time: 2 hours

Servings: 2

Ingredients

- 5 cups of BBQ sauce
- 5 cups of grape jelly
- 12 oz of frozen meatballs

Instructions

- Layer meatballs with BBQ sauce and grape jelly into the bottom of the crockpot.

- Cook for 2-4 hours on low.
- Stir well and top with some chopped parsley.

Nutrients: Kcal: 310, Fats: 19 g, Total Carbs: 17 g, Proteins: 15 g.

11. Crockpot Boiled Peanuts

Prep Time: 10 minutes

Cook Time: 6 hours

Servings: 2

Ingredients

- ½ cup of salt
- 2 ½ cups of water
- 10 oz of dried raw peanuts in the shell

Instructions

- Add rinsed peanuts with all ingredients to the crockpot.
- Cook for 5 hours on low.
- Remove excess water and serve.

Nutrients: Kcal: 214, Fats: 19 g, Total Carbs: 6 g, Proteins: 10 g.

12. Stuffed Mushroom with Ranch & Bacon

Prep Time: 10 minutes

Cook Time: 5 hours

Servings: 2

Ingredients

- 2-3 tbsp of butter
- 2 tbsp of Ranch Dressing mix
- 1 tbsp of Worcestershire sauce
- 1 cup of cream cheese, softened
- 2 cups of bacon, cooked
- 20-25 mushrooms

Instructions

- Combine all ingredients with diced mushrooms except butter and sauces.

- Grease the crockpot with some butter and add coated mushrooms.
- Cook for 1 hour on low.
- Stir in the Worcestershire sauce and bacon to the mushrooms and cook for 3 hours on low.

Nutrients: Kcal: 347, Fats: 34 g, Total Carbs: 28 g, Proteins: 16 g.

13. Nuts & Bolts Snack Mix

Prep Time: 10 minutes

Cook Time: 2 hours

Servings: 2

Ingredients

- 1 cup of salted butter
- 1-2 tsp of seasoning salt
- 1 tsp of smoked paprika
- 1 tsp of onion powder
- 1 ½ tsp of garlic powder
- 1 cup of plain crackers
- 2 tbsp of Worcestershire Sauce
- 1 cup of pecans
- 2 cups of pretzels
- 3 cups of pretzel sticks
- 2 cups of roasted salted peanuts
- 3 cups of cheerios cereal
- 4 cups of Chex cereal

Instructions

- Mix all sauces in a bowl.
- Add all cereals and nuts to the crockpot.
- Pour the sauce mixture over the cereals and toss well.
- Cook for 2-3 hours on low.

Nutrients: Kcal: 197, Fats: 13 g, Total Carbs: 17 g, Proteins: 5 g.

14. BBQ Little Smokies

Prep Time: 5 minutes

Cook Time: 3 hours

Servings: 2

Ingredients

- 3/4 cup of grape jelly
- 1 cup of BBQ sauce
- 10 oz of Little Smokies

Instructions

- Fry the smokies in some oil.
- Spoon sauce with grape jelly over the smokies.
- Ladle the smokies to the crockpot.
- Cook for 2-3 hours on low or 1 hour on high.

Nutrients: Kcal: 313, Fats: 19 g, Total Carbs: 25 g, Proteins: 9 g.

15. Crockpot Chex Mix

Prep Time: 5 minutes

Cook Time: 2 hours 5 minutes

Servings: 2

Ingredients

- 1 ½ tsp of seasoned salt
- ½ tsp of onion powder
- ¾ tsp of garlic powder
- 2 tbsp of Worcestershire sauce
- 6 tbsp of butter, melted
- 3 cups of corn Chex cereal
- 2 cups wheat Chex cereal
- 3 cups rice Chex cereal
- 2 cups bite-size pretzels

Instructions

- Combine butter with all sauces and spices in a bowl.

- Add cereal and pretzels to the crockpot.
- Pour the prepared mixture over the cereals.
- Cook for 2 hours on high.

Nutrients: Kcal: 100, Fats: 1 g, Total Carbs: 15 g, Proteins: 1 g.

16. Santa Fe Chicken

Prep Time: 5 minutes

Cook Time: 8 hours

Servings: 2

Ingredients

- 1 tsp of salt
- 1 tsp of cayenne pepper
- 1 tsp of cumin
- 1 tsp of onion powder
- 1 tsp of garlic powder
- ¼ cup of chopped fresh cilantro
- 2 cups of chicken broth
- 3 scallions, chopped
- 1 cup of black beans
- 8 oz of frozen corn
- 5 oz of diced tomatoes with mild green chilies
- 12-14 oz of chicken breast

Instructions

- Coat chicken breasts with salt and pepper.
- Add all ingredients to the crockpot. Layer the chicken breasts on top.
- Cook for 4-6 hours on high. Shred the chicken on a separate plate.
- Serve with cooked rice.

Nutrients: Kcal: 183, Fats: 3 g, Total Carbs: 17 g, Proteins: 24 g.

17. Cocktail Smokies

Prep Time: 5 minutes

Cook Time: 2 hours

Servings: 2

Ingredients

- 8 oz of jar grape jelly
- 10 oz of barbeque sauce
- 10 oz of miniature smoked sausage

Instructions

- Mix BBQ sauce with smoked sausages and grape jelly in the crockpot.
- Cook for 2-3 hours on high.

Nutrients: Kcal: 246, Fats: 22 g, Total Carbs: 28 g, Proteins: 10 g.

18. Ro-Tel Dip with Ground Beef & Cheese

Prep Time: 10 minutes

Cook Time: 1 hour 30 minutes

Servings: 2

Ingredients

- ¼ cup of finely chopped onion
- 10 oz of Velveeta, shredded
- 1-2 oz of tomatoes with green chiles
- ½ cup of mild green chiles, chopped
- 1 cup of sliced mushrooms
- 10 oz of lean ground beef

Instructions

- Mix tomatoes with green chiles and Velveeta in the bowl.
- Sauté beef with onions in the crockpot.
- Add mushrooms, cheese and peppers. Cook for 30 minutes on low.
- Ladle the Velveeta mixture into the pot and cook for 1 hour. Serve with crackers.

Nutrients: Kcal: 347, Fats: 34 g, Total Carbs: 28 g, Proteins: 16 g.

19. Kielbasa Sausage Bites

Prep Time: 10 minutes

Cook Time: 6 hours

Servings: 2

Ingredients

- 2 tbsp of brown sugar
- 2 tbsp of honey
- 1 tbsp of red pepper flakes
- 2 cups of BBQ sauce
- 1 cup of jar red pepper jelly
- 2-3 cups of kielbasa

Instructions

- Add all ingredients to the crockpot.
- Cook for 6 hours on low.
- Toss well before serving.

Nutrients: Kcal: 653, Fats: 41 g, Total Carbs: 49 g, Proteins: 21 g.

20. Bourbon Glazed Kielbasa

Prep Time: 30 minutes

Cook Time: 4 hours

Servings: 2

Ingredients

- 10 oz of kielbasa sausage
- 2 tbsp of bourbon
- ½ cup of maple syrup
- 1 cup of apricot preserves

Instructions

- Add all ingredients to the crockpot.
- Cook for 4 hours on low or 2 hours on high.
- Add desired toppings before serving.

Nutrients: Kcal: 212, Fats: 5 g, Total Carbs: 38

g, Proteins: 8 g.

21. Sweet Chili BBQ Kielbasa

Prep Time: 15 minutes

Cook Time: 2 hours

Servings: 2

Ingredients

- 1 cup of BBQ sauce
- 1 cup of sweet chili sauce
- 8 oz of kielbasa

Instructions

- Combine BBQ sauce with sweet chili sauce with kielbasa and toss well.
- Transfer the kielbasa mixture to the crockpot.
- Cook for 3-4 hours on low until thickened.

Nutrients: Kcal: 198, Fats: 15 g, Total Carbs: 27 g, Proteins: 22 g.

22. Chipotle Brisket Sliders

Prep Time: 10 minutes

Cook Time: 4 hours

Servings: 2

Ingredients

- 2 tsp of kosher salt
- ¾ tsp of black pepper
- 1 tsp of ground cumin
- 1 ½ tbsp of brown sugar
- 3 garlic cloves, minced
- 1 cup of barbecue sauce
- 2 tbsp of chipotle chiles in adobo sauce, minced
- ½ cup of spicy pickle chips
- 10 oz of beef brisket
- 4-6 slider buns, toasted

Instructions

- Mix all spices in a bowl. Coat brisket with spice mixture and remaining ingredients.
- Transfer the brisket mixture to the crockpot.
- Cook for 3-4 hours on high or 6 hours on low.
- Slice the brisket on a plate. Layer the sliced briskets with sauce and toppings on a bun.

Nutrients: Kcal: 284, Fats: 29 g, Total Carbs: 23.1 g, Proteins: 19 g.

23. Green Bean Chips

Prep Time: 5 minutes

Cook Time: 12 hours

Servings: 2

Ingredients

- 1 tsp of salt
- 2 lb of green beans
- 1/2 cup of oil
- 1/6 cup of yeast

Instructions

- Add everything to the crockpot.
- Cook at low for about 12 hours.

Nutrients: Kcal: 140, Fats: 6 g, Total Carbs: 15 g, Proteins: 1 g

24. Cheesy Spaghetti Squash

Prep Time: 15 minutes

Cook Time: 4 hours

Servings: 2

Ingredients

- 1 tsp of salt
- 1 spaghetti squash, cut
- 3/4 cup of mozzarella, shredded
- 1/4 cup of butter
- 1 ½ oz Parmesan cheese. grated
- 2 minced garlic cloves
- 1 ½ oz Asiago cheese. grated
- ½ tsp of pepper
- ¼ cup of fresh basil, chopped

Instructions

- Cook squash in the crockpot at low for about 4 hours.
- Add all other ingredients to the crockpot. Cook for 10 minutes.
- Top with basil leaves and serve.

Nutrients: Kcal: 192, Fats: 14 g, Total Carbs: 6 g, Proteins: 8 g

25. Ranch Crackers

Prep Time: 5 minutes

Cook Time: 30 minutes

Servings: 2

Ingredients

- ½ tsp of minced garlic
- 4 oz of oyster crackers
- ¼ cup of oil
- 1 oz of dry ranch dressing

Instructions

- Mix everything except crackers in a bowl.
- Coat crackers with this mixture.
- Add to the crockpot and cook at low for 30 minutes.
- Serve and enjoy.

Nutrients: Kcal: 402, Fats: 17 g, Total Carbs: 59 g, Proteins: 5 g

26. Bacon, Garlic & Sweet Green Beans

Prep Time: 10 minutes

Cook Time: 5 hours

Servings: 2

Ingredients

- 1/3 cup of brown sugar
- 5 oz of green beans
- ½ cup of butter
- 4 garlic cloves, minced
- ½ lb of bacon diced, uncooked

Instructions

- Add everything to the crockpot.
- Cook at high for 1 hour and then at low for 4 hours.

Nutrients: Kcal: 281, Fats: 15 g, Total Carbs: 20 g, Proteins: 12 g

27. Sweet Acorn Squash

Prep Time: 10 min

Cook Time: 3 hrs

Servings: 2

Ingredients

- 1 tbsp of Brown Sugar
- 1/2 Acorn Squash, cut, seeds removed
- 1 tbsp of Butter

Instructions

- Add everything to the crockpot.
- Cook at high for three hours.

Nutrients: Kcal: 124, Fats: 6 g, Total Carbs: 18 g, Proteins: 1 g

28. Vegetable Medley

Prep Time: 15 minutes

Cook Time: 6 hours

Servings: 2

Ingredients

- 1/2 cup of broccoli florets, cut
- ½ tsp of salt
- 1 sliced tomato
- ¼ cup of water
- 1 tbsp of coconut spread butter
- 1/2 lb of white mushrooms
- 1 red onion, sliced
- 1/2 tsp of garlic powder
- ½ tsp of pepper

Instructions

- Add everything to the crockpot.
- Cook at low for about six hours.

Nutrients: Kcal: 114, Fats: 6 g, Total Carbs: 12 g, Proteins: 5g

Chapter 15: Staples & Sauces

1. Jalapeño Corn Dip

Prep Time: 5 minutes

Cook Time: 2 hours

Servings: 2

Ingredients

- 1 cup of shredded Colby Jack cheese
- 1 lime
- 1 cup of cream cheese, cubed
- ⅔ cup of sour cream
- ¼ cup of chopped cilantro
- 2 jalapeños
- 6 slices of bacon, cooked
- ¼ cup of crumbled queso fresco
- 2 cups of whole-kernel corn

Instructions

- Add all ingredients to the crockpot except bacon.
- Cook for 2 hours on low. Stir in bacon and cook for 5 minutes.
- Season with salt and pepper.
- Top with some queso fresco before serving.

Nutrients: Kcal: 347, Fats: 34 g, Total Carbs: 28 g, Proteins: 16 g.

2. Buffalo Chicken Dip

Prep Time: 7 minutes

Cook Time: 2 hours

Servings: 2

Ingredients

- ½ cup of reduced-fat cream cheese
- ½ cup of diced celery
- ¼ cup of cayenne pepper sauce
- 1 1/3 cups of shredded boneless chicken breast
- ¼ cup of diced sweet onion
- 6 tbsp of reduced-fat Greek yogurt
- 1 cup of reduced-fat, shredded cheddar cheese

Instructions

- Add all ingredients to the crockpot except onion and celery.
- Cook for 2 hours on low.
- Stir in chopped green onions and celery.
- Cook for 5 minutes and top with cheddar cheese.

Nutrients: Kcal: 60, Fats: 4 g, Total Carbs: 1 g, Proteins: 5 g.

3. Spinach & Artichoke Dip

Prep Time: 5 minutes

Cook Time: 1 hour 5 minutes

Servings: 2

Ingredients

- 2 tsp of minced garlic
- 1/3 cup of mayonnaise
- 14 oz of artichoke hearts, chopped
- 8 oz of softened cheese
- 2/3 cup of sour cream
- 10 oz of frozen chopped spinach

- 2 cups of Parmesan cheese, shredded

Instructions

- Mix all sauce ingredients in a bowl.
- Pour this mixture over spinach, artichoke and parmesan cheese in the crockpot.
- Cook for 1 hour on high or 3 hours on low.

Nutrients: Kcal: 225, Fats: 25 g, Total Carbs: 10 g, Proteins: 5 g.

4. Taco Dip

Prep Time: 10 minutes

Cook Time: 3 hours

Servings: 2

Ingredients

- 2 tbsp of taco seasoning
- 1 cup of diced tomatoes & green chiles
- 1 yellow onion, diced
- 1 jalapeno, diced
- ½ cup of reduced-sodium beef broth
- 1 poblano pepper, diced
- 2 tbsp of cornstarch
- 1 cup of shredded Mexican blend cheese
- 5 oz of ground beef

Instructions

- Sauté beef in olive oil for 5 minutes, until browned.
- Sauté jalapeno, poblano and onions for 4 minutes.
- Add all ingredients to the crockpot and toss well.
- Cook for 3 hours on low.
- Add cheese on top and let it melt for 10 minutes.

Nutrients: Kcal: 138, Fats: 4 g, Total Carbs: 8

g, Proteins: 6 g.

5. Corn Dip

Prep Time: 5 minutes

Cook Time: 2 hours

Servings: 2

Ingredients

- 1 tsp of kosher salt
- ½ tsp of garlic powder
- ½ cup of milk
- ½ cup of chopped green onions
- 1 tsp of ground black pepper
- 3 oz of cream cheese
- 1 jalapeno, finely chopped
- 4 cups of frozen corn

Instructions

- Put all ingredients into the crockpot.
- Cook for 1 hour on high.
- Add chopped green onions on top and serve.

Nutrients: Kcal: 157, Fats: 8 g, Total Carbs: 18 g, Proteins: 3 g.

6. Cheese Dip

Prep Time: 10 minutes

Cook Time: 2 hours 5 minutes

Servings: 2

Ingredients

- ½ cup of ranch dip
- 4 slices of bacon, cooked
- 4 oz of cream cheese, cubed
- 1 cup of shredded cheddar cheese
- 1 cup of sour cream

Instructions

- Combine all ingredients and add to the crockpot.

- Cook for 2 hours on low.
- Top with shredded cheese before serving.

Nutrients: Kcal: 320, Fats: 14 g, Total Carbs: 4 g, Proteins: 9 g.

7. Reuben Dip

Prep Time: 10 minutes

Cook Time: 2 hours

Servings: 2

Ingredients

- ¼ tsp of thousand island dressing
- 4 oz of plain cream cheese, softened
- ½ cup of sauerkraut, drained
- ½ cup of sour cream
- 1 ¼ cups of Swiss cheese, grated
- 4 oz of sliced corned beef, chopped

Instructions

- Add all ingredients to the crockpot.
- Cook for 2 hours on high.
- Top with shredded cheese and let it melt.

Nutrients: Kcal: 197, Fats: 34 g, Total Carbs: 19 g, Proteins: 26 g.

8. 7-Layer Bean Dip

Prep Time: 20 minutes

Cook Time: 2 hours

Servings: 2

Ingredients

- 10 oz of ground beef
- ½ tsp of salt
- ¼ cup of green onions, sliced
- ½ tsp of garlic powder
- 8 oz of cheddar cheese, shredded
- ¼ tsp of pepper

- 2 ½ cups of refried beans
- 1 cup of salsa
- ½ cup of jarred jalapeno slices
- 1 cup of sour cream

Instructions

- Season beef with salt, pepper and garlic powder.
- Sauté beef for 5 minutes on both sides.
- Layer beans with beef in the bottom of the crockpot. Add remaining ingredients on top.
- Cook for 2 hours on low.

Nutrients: Kcal: 319, Fats: 21 g, Total Carbs: 10 g, Proteins: 22 g.

9. White Queso Dip

Prep Time: 10 minutes

Cook Time: 1 hour

Servings: 2

Ingredients

- 2 oz of cream cheese
- 1 cup of cheddar cheese
- 3 oz of green chilies and Rotel tomatoes, canned
- 1 cup of mozzarella cheese
- 4 oz of sour cream
- ¾ cup of heavy cream

Instructions

- Add all ingredients to the crockpot.
- Cook at low for an hour.
- Serve warm.

Nutrients: Kcal: 549, Fats: 49 g, Total Carbs: 5 g, Proteins: 23 g.

10. Spaghetti Sauce

Prep Time: 15 minutes

Cook Time: 8 hours

Servings: 2

Ingredients

- ½ crushed tomatoes can
- ¼ cup of olive oil
- pepper to taste
- 1 oz of sliced salt pork
- 1/3 tsp of dried oregano
- 1 tbsp of minced onion
- 2 fresh basil leaves
- ½ tsp of salt
- 2 cloves of garlic, minced
- 1/2 lb of minced beef

Instructions

- In heated oil, cook pork.
- Then saute onion and garlic separately.
- Add everything to the crockpot.
- Cook at low for 8 hours.

Nutrients: Kcal: 144, Fats: 12 g, Total Carbs: 5 g, Proteins: 6 g.

11. Pumpkin Butter

Prep Time: 5 minutes

Cook Time: 3 hours

Servings: 2

Ingredients

- 1 oz of pumpkin
- ½ tsp of ginger
- 1/3 cup of sweetener
- ¼ tsp of nutmeg
- 1/3 cup of alternative brown sugar
- ¼ tsp of cinnamon

- 1/8 tsp of cloves

Instructions

- Add everything to the crockpot.
- Cook at low for 3 hours.

Nutrients: Kcal: 4, Fats: 1 g, Total Carbs: 1 g, Proteins: 1 g.

12. Tasty Cabbage

Prep Time: 10 minutes

Cook Time: 6 hours

Servings: 2

Ingredients

- 2 cups of broth
- 1 chopped cabbage, cored
- salt as per taste
- 1/3 cup chopped bacon
- ¼ cup of sliced butter
- pepper as per taste
- 2 oz of pearl onion jar

Instructions

- Add everything to the crockpot.
- Cook at low for 6 hours.

Nutrients: Kcal: 52, Fats: 2 g, Total Carbs: 4 g, Proteins: 1 g.

13. Banana Jam

Prep Time: 10 minutes

Cook Time: 2 hours

Servings: 2

Ingredients

- 1 cup of sugar
- 2 medium mashed bananas
- 1 tbsp of lemon juice

Instructions

- Add everything to the crockpot.
- Cook at low for 2 hours.

- Set aside to cool.
- Store in an airtight container for later use.

Nutrients: Kcal: 67, Fats: 0.04 g, Total Carbs: 17 g, Proteins: 0.1 g.

14. Caramel Apple Butter

Prep Time: 30 minutes

Cook Time: 6 hours

Servings: 2

Ingredients

- 1 oz of caramels
- ½ lb of quartered apples
- 1/3 tsp of ground cinnamon
- 1/3 cup of cider vinegar
- 1/3 tsp of ground cloves

Instructions

- Add apples and cider vinegar to the crockpot.
- Cook at low for 5 hours.
- Add this into the blender and process well.
- Add apple puree back to the crockpot with all other ingredients. Mix and cook for 1 hour.
- Store in an airtight container for later use.

Nutrients: Kcal: 11, Fats: 0.2 g, Total Carbs: 2 g, Proteins: 0.1 g.

15. Homemade Chicken Broth

Prep Time: 5 minutes

Cook Time: 6 hours

Servings: 2

Ingredients

- 2 cups of water
- Skin & bones of cooked chicken

Instructions

- Add everything to the crockpot.
- Cook at low for 6 hours.
- Strain the liquid and remove fat.

Nutrients: Kcal: 12, Fats: 0 g, Total Carbs: 1 g, Proteins: 2 g.

16. Tomato Sauce

Prep Time: 20 minutes

Cook Time: 11 hours

Servings: 2

Ingredients

- 1 lb of fresh tomatoes
- 2 oz of lemon juice

Instructions

- Add tomatoes to the crockpot. Cook at low for 2 hours.
- Blend the cooked tomatoes in a blender.
- Add tomato puree back to the crockpot and cook at low for about 8 hours.
- Pour sauce into jars and add lemon juice on top.
- Cover and store in an airtight jar.

Nutrients: Kcal: 34, Fats: 0.4 g, Total Carbs: 8 g, Proteins: 1 g.

17. Chili Coney Dog Sauce

Prep Time: 20 minutes

Cook Time: 4 hours

Servings: 2

Ingredients

- 1/2 lb of minced beef
- ½ tsp of chili powder
- 2 oz of tomato sauce
- ½ tsp of garlic powder
- ½ cup of water

- ½ tsp of ground mustard
- 1 ½ tsp of Worcestershire sauce
- ¼ cup of onion
- ½ tsp of black pepper
- 1/8 tsp of cayenne pepper

Instructions

- Cook beef in a pan until brown.
- Add everything to the crockpot.
- Cook at low for about 4 hours.

Nutrients: Kcal: 112, Fats: 4 g, Total Carbs: 5 g, Proteins: 12 g.

18. Marinara Sauce

Prep Time: 15 minutes

Cook Time: 4 hours

Servings: 2

Ingredients

- 2 cloves of garlic, minced
- 1/2 tbsp of Italian seasoning
- 4 oz of diced tomatoes, canned
- 1/2 tbsp of minced basil
- 4 oz of canned crushed tomatoes
- 1/2 tbsp of onion powder
- 1/2 tbsp of tomato paste, canned
- 1/2 tsp of balsamic vinegar

Instructions

- Add everything to the crockpot.
- Cook at low for about 4 hours.
- Store in the fridge for later use.

Nutrients: Kcal: 29, Fats: 0.1 g, Total Carbs: 6 g, Proteins: 1 g.

19. Pizza Sauce

Prep Time: 15 minutes

Cook Time: 6 hours

Servings: 2

Ingredients

- 1/2 tsp of dried oregano
- 2 oz of tomato sauce, canned
- 1/2 tsp of kosher salt
- 1 tbsp of tomato paste ,canned
- 1/2 tsp of granulated sugar
- 1/2 tsp of dried basil
- 1/2 tsp of garlic powder
- 1/2 tsp of black pepper

Instructions

- Add everything to the crockpot.
- Cook at low for about 6 hours.

Nutrients: Kcal: 40, Fats: 0.4 g, Total Carbs: 9 g, Proteins: 2 g.

20. Turkey Bolognese Sauce

Prep Time: 45 minutes

Cook Time: 6 hours

Servings: 2

Ingredients

- 1/2 medium yellow onion, diced
- 2 oz of crushed tomatoes, canned
- 1 medium carrot, diced

- 1/2 medium bell pepper, diced
- ½ tsp of dried rosemary
- 1 clove of garlic, minced
- 1/2 tsp of dried oregano
- ½ lb of minced turkey
- ½ tsp of fennel seeds
- 2 oz of tomato paste, canned
- 1/2 tsp of black pepper
- 1 rib of celery, diced
- ½ tsp of crushed pepper flakes
- 1 tsp of granulated sugar

Instructions

- Saute all veggies in a pan.
- Cook turkey until brown.
- Add everything to the crockpot.
- Cook at low for about 6 hours.

Nutrients: Kcal: 133, Fats: 2 g, Total Carbs: 12 g, Proteins: 20 g.

21. Veggie Loaded Spaghetti Sauce

Prep Time: 20 minutes

Cook Time: 10 hours

Servings: 2

Ingredients

- 1 diced onion
- 1 crumbled bay leaf
- 2 diced carrots
- 1 tsp of dried oregano
- 2 diced bell peppers
- 1 oz of crushed tomatoes
- 2 small diced zucchini
- 1/2 tsp of dried rosemary
- 1 cup of chopped mushrooms
- 2 garlic cloves, minced

- 1/2 tsp of basil

Instructions

- Add everything to the crockpot.
- Cook at low for about 10 hours.

Nutrients: Kcal: 43, Fats: 0.5 g, Total Carbs: 10 g, Proteins: 2 g.

22. Pumpkin Puree

Prep Time: 15 minutes

Cook Time: 8 hours

Servings: 2

Ingredients

- 1/2 fresh medium pie pumpkin, cut, seeds removed

Instructions

- Add it to the crockpot.
- Cook at low for 8 hours.
- Blend it in the processor. Pour it into a dish.
- Freeze and use later.

Nutrients: Kcal: 26, Fats: 0.1 g, Total Carbs: 7 g, Proteins: 1 g.

23. Pork & BBQ Sauce

Prep Time: 15 minutes

Cook Time: 9 hours

Servings: 2

Ingredients

- 1/2 tsp of powdered onion
- 1 tsp of sea salt
- 1/2 large onion, diced
- ½ tsp of paprika
- 1 fresh bay leaf
- ½ tsp of powdered garlic
- 1/2 tsp of smoked paprika
- 1/4 cup of spicy BBQ sauce

- ½ tsp white or black pepper

Instructions

- Add everything to the crockpot.
- Cook at low for about 9 hours.

Nutrients: Kcal: 497, Fats: 35 g, Total Carbs: 3 g, Proteins: 35 g.

24. Roast & Peanut Sauce

Prep Time: 15 minutes

Cook Time: 3 hours

Servings: 2

Ingredients

- ¼ cup of peanut butter
- 1/4 cup chicken stock
- 1 tbsp of sweetener
- 1/2 tbsp of fresh ginger, minced
- ¼ cup of tomato sauce
- 1/2 tbsp of minced garlic
- 1 tbsp of soy sauce
- 1 tsp of garlic chile paste

Instructions

- Blend everything, add to the crockpot and cook at low for 3 hours.
- Serve with meat and other dishes.

Nutrients: Kcal: 583, Fats: 25 g, Total Carbs: 3 g, Proteins: 76 g.

25. Italian Chicken & Cauliflower

Prep Time: 5 minutes

Cook Time: 4 hours

Servings: 2

Ingredients

- 1 cup of chopped cauliflower
- 1 lb of chicken breast
- 2 oz of sliced button mushrooms
- 1 pack of Italian dressing mix for salad

- 2 oz of sliced cream cheese

Instructions

- Add everything except cream cheese to the crockpot.
- Cook at low for 6 hours and at high for 4 hours.
- Shred chicken, add it back to the crockpot, mix cream cheese into it.
- Top with parsley and serve.

Nutrients: Kcal: 467, Fats: 28 g, Total Carbs: 5 g, Proteins: 44 g.

26. Overnight Oatmeal

Prep Time: 5 minutes

Cook Time: 6 hours

Servings: 2

Ingredients

- 1 cup of oats
- 1 tbsp of shredded sweetened coconut
- 2 cups of water
- ¼ cup of cocoa powder, unsweetened
- 1 oz can of coconut milk
- 2 tbsp of brown sugar
- Chopped pecans

Instructions

- Put all the ingredients into the crockpot.
- Cook at low for 6 hours.
- Add cocoa on top and serve.

Nutrients: Kcal: 267, Fats: 8 g, Total Carbs: 39 g, Proteins: 9 g.

Chapter 16: Vegetarian Recipes

1. Cabbage & Onions

Prep time: 15 minutes

Cook time: 6 hours

Servings: 2

Ingredients

- 1/2 tsp of mustard powder
- 2 cups of sliced onions
- 1/4 cup of broth
- 3 cups of chopped cabbage
- 1/2 tsp of black pepper
- 1 tbsp of EVOO
- 1 tsp cumin powder
- 1 tsp of garlic minced
- 1/2 tsp of salt

Instructions

- Add all the ingredients to the crockpot & cook at low for about six hours.

Nutrients: Kcal 52, Fats: 2g, Total Carbs: 4g, Proteins: 1g

2. Cauliflower Mash

Prep time: 10 minutes

Cook time: 6 hours

Servings: 2

Ingredients

- 1 cup of veggie broth
- 1 tsp of sea salt
- 1 head of cauliflower florets, chopped
- 2 tbsp of ghee
- 2 cloves of peeled garlic
- 2 cups of water
- 1 tbsp of fresh herbs

Instructions

- Add all the ingredients to the crockpot except ghee, herbs & cook at low for about six hours.
- Drain it well.
- Then add the rest of the ingredients and blend until smooth.
- Season it and enjoy.

Nutrients: Kcal 108, Fats: 7g, Total Carbs: 6g, Proteins: 2g

3. Cauliflower & Lentil Curry

Prep time: 15 minutes

Cook time: 7 hours

Servings: 2

Ingredients

- 1/2 tsp of ground cumin
- 1 cup of red lentils
- 1/2 tsp of ground coriander
- 1 yellow onion, diced
- 1/2 tsp of ground turmeric
- 1 clove of garlic, minced
- 1 tsp of salt

- 1/4 tsp of ground cardamom
- 1 head of cauliflower, chopped
- 1 tbsp of curry paste
- 1/2 cup of coconut milk
- 1/2 tbsp of minced ginger
- 1 cup of brown rice to serve
- 1/2 tsp of cayenne pepper
- 5 ounces of tomato puree, canned
- fresh cilantro, chopped

Instructions

- Add all the ingredients to the crockpot except coconut milk.
- Cook at low for about seven hours.
- Once done, add the coconut milk and mix well.
- Serve and enjoy.

Nutrients: Kcal 199, Fats: 1g, Total Carbs: 39g, Proteins: 6g

4. Loaded Sweet Potatoes

Prep time: 10 minutes

Cook time: 3 hours

Servings: 2

Ingredients

- 2 sweet potatoes, medium
- 2 tbsp of cilantro, chopped
- ½ cup of black beans, canned
- ½ tsp of cumin
- ½ cup of fresh corn, fresh or frozen
- 1/3 cup of tomato sauce
- ½ tsp of kosher salt
- 2 tbsp of scallions, chopped
- ¼ tsp of cayenne pepper
- 1/2 chopped avocado

For Cashew Cream:

- ¼ tsp of salt
- ½ cup of raw soaked cashews, soaked for half hour
- 1–2 tsp of hot sauce
- ½ cup of water
- ¼ tsp of smoked paprika
- ½ tsp of lemon juice

Instructions

- Cook the sweet potatoes in the crockpot at high for three hours.
- Mix beans, salt, tomato sauce, cumin, cayenne & corn in a bowl.
- Blend the drained cashews, add all other cashew cream ingredients, mix well & put aside.
- Once done, slit sweet potatoes and pour the mixture into them. Add cashew cream on top and serve.

Nutrients: Kcal 221, Fats: 5g, Total Carbs: 35g, Proteins: 9g

5. Thai Veggie Curry

Prep time: 45 minutes

Cook time: 4 hours

Servings: 2

Ingredients

- 2 tsp of Sriracha sauce
- ½ cauliflower head florets, cut
- 2 cups of prepared brown rice
- 2 medium cubed sweet potatoes
- 1/4 cup of chopped fresh cilantro
- 1 small diced onion
- 1 cup of green peas
- 14 oz of coconut milk, canned
- 1 tbsp of brown sugar
- 3 tbsp of soy sauce

- ½ tsp of salt
- 1.5 tbsp of curry paste
- 4 oz of white mushrooms
- ½ cup of toasted cashews
- fresh basil leaves

Instructions

- Toast cashews in the microwave for about five minutes.
- Add coconut milk, soy sauce, salt, curry paste, and brown sugar, then sriracha to a bowl. Mix well.
- Add this mixture to the crockpot and cook at low for about four hours.
- Then add in the peas & mushrooms. Cook for about thirty more minutes and serve.

Nutrients: Kcal 82, Fats: 2g, Total Carbs: 13g, Proteins: 3g

6. Chickpeas & Veggies Over Quinoa

Prep time: 15 minutes

Cook time: 5 hours

Servings: 2

Ingredients

- 3 carrots, diced
- 3 cups of quinoa cooked
- 1 cup of chickpeas, soaked in water with 1 tsp of baking soda
- 2 potatoes, diced
- 1 onion, diced

For the Sauce:

- 3 tsp of crushed garlic
- 1 tsp of crushed pepper
- 2 tbsp of sesame oil
- 2 tbsp of paprika
- 2 tbsp of rice vinegar
- 1 tbsp of miso

- 5 tbsp of soy sauce
- 3 tbsp of maple syrup
- 4 tbsp of mirin

Garnish:

- 3 sliced green onions
- Sesame seeds

Instructions

- Add the rinsed beans to the crockpot with all the veggies. Cook at high for about 5 hours.
- Blend the sauce ingredients and pour into the crockpot.
- Mix and serve.

Nutrients: Kcal 455, Fats: 9g, Total Carbs: 80g, Proteins: 16g

7. Vegan Rice & Beans

Prep time: 5 minutes

Cook time: 4 hours

Servings: 2

Ingredients

- 3 tbsp of olive oil
- 1 (6 oz) pack of cauliflower rice
- 1 tbsp of Mexican oregano
- 1 can of black soy
- 1 tsp of chili powder
- ½ cup of hemp seeds
- 1 tsp of onion powder
- 1 cup of stock or broth
- 2 tsp of garlic powder
- 1 tsp of cumin
- ½ tsp of cayenne powder

Instructions

- Add everything to the crockpot except oregano.
- Cook at high for about 4 hours.

- Once done, add oregano on top and serve.

Nutrients: Kcal 299, Fats: 20g, Total Carbs: 5g, Proteins: 19g

8. Black Beans With Pumpkin & Chili

Prep time: 10 minutes

Cook time: 8 hours

Servings: 2

Ingredients

- 1 tsp of cinnamon
- 7 oz of black beans
- ½ tsp of black pepper
- 1 can of diced tomatoes
- 1/8 tsp of ground cloves
- 1 cup of pumpkin, pureed
- 2 cups of yellow onion, diced
- 1 tsp of cumin
- 1 medium yellow bell pepper, diced
- ¼ tsp of nutmeg
- ½ tsp of kosher salt
- ½ tbsp of chili powder
- Assorted toppings

Instructions

- Add everything to the crockpot & cook at low for about eight hours.
- Serve and enjoy.

Nutrients: Kcal 295, Fats: 15g, Total Carbs: 25g, Proteins: 15g

9. Red Lentil Curry

Prep time: 20 minutes

Cook time: 8 hours

Servings: 2

Ingredients

- 1 tsp of garam masala
- 1 cup of brown lentils
- ½ cup of coconut milk
- 1 diced onions
- 1 tsp of cayenne pepper
- 2 cloves of garlic, minced
- 1 tsp of sugar
- 1/2 tbsp of minced ginger
- 2.5 tbsp of curry paste
- ½ tsp of turmeric
- 1 can of tomato puree
- cilantro to garnish
- 1 tsp of salt
- Cooked brown rice to serve

Instructions

- Add lentils, spices, tomato puree and water to the crockpot.
- Cook at low for about 8 hours.
- Once done, add coconut milk and top with cilantro.
- Serve with rice.

Nutrients: Kcal 250, Fats: 3g, Total Carbs: 42g, Proteins: 15g

10. Chickpeas & Red Potatoes

Prep time: 20 minutes

Cook time: 4 hours

Servings: 2

Ingredients

- 2 tsp of olive oil
- 1 lime
- 1 diced yellow onion
- 1/2 lb of diced red potatoes
- 1 clove of garlic, minced
- 1 cup veggie broth
- 1 tsp of ground coriander

- 1 tsp of kosher salt
- 2 tsp of ground cumin
- 1/4 tsp of turmeric
- 6 oz of diced tomatoes, canned
- 1/2 tsp of garam masala
- 2 tbsp of tomato paste
- 1/4 tsp of crushed pepper flakes
- 6 oz of chickpeas, canned
- 1/2 tsp of ground ginger
- fresh cilantro

Instructions

- Sauté onion in a pan for about five minutes.
- Add remaining ingredients to the pan except for potatoes & chickpeas. Cook for some time.
- Then transfer everything to the crockpot and cook at high for about four hours.
- Top with cilantro and serve.

Nutrients: Kcal 418, Fats: 15g, Total Carbs: 62g, Proteins: 19g

11. Shakshuka

Prep time: 10 minutes

Cook time: 2 hours

Servings: 2

Ingredients

- 1 small onion, chopped
- 2 eggs
- 1 tsp of cumin
- 2 tsp of oil
- 2 diced tomatoes
- ½ tsp of paprika
- 2 garlic cloves, minced
- ½ tsp of pepper

- 1 bell pepper, chopped
- 1 tsp of salt
- ½ tsp of coriander
- A handful of chopped parsley

Instructions

- Mix all ingredients except for the eggs in a bowl.
- Cook at high for about two hours.
- Now make two holes in shakshuka mixture & add one egg per hole.
- Cook till done and serve.

Nutrients: Kcal 132, Fats: 5g, Total Carbs: 11g, Proteins: 7g

12. Chickpeas & Potato Curry

Prep time: 25 minutes

Cook time: 4 hours

Servings: 2

Ingredients

- 1/2 tsp of salt
- 1 tbsp of canola oil
- 1/2 tsp of garam masala
- fresh chopped cilantro
- 1 chopped onion
- 1 cup of veggie stock
- 2 garlic cloves, minced
- 10 oz of drained, rinsed chickpeas
- 2 tsp of fresh minced ginger root
- 1/4 tsp of ground turmeric
- 1 tsp of ground coriander
- 1 tsp of chili powder
- 1/2 tsp of ground cumin
- 5 oz of crushed tomatoes
- 1 large peeled & cubed baking potato
- 1 tsp of lime juice

- cooked rice

Instructions

- Sauté onion with minced garlic, dry seasoning & ginger in a pan for about 2 minutes.
- Add tomatoes & put them in the crockpot.
- Then add stock, potato cubes & chickpeas.
- Cook at low for about 4 hours.
- Top with some cilantro and lime juice. Serve.

Nutrients: Kcal 240, Fats: 6g, Total Carbs: 42g, Proteins: 8g

13. Crockpot Ratatouille

Prep time: 30 minutes

Cook time: 4 hours

Servings: 2

Ingredients

- 2 large bell peppers, diced
- 2 tbsp of olive oil
- ½ tsp of salt
- 2 diced yellow onions
- 2 garlic cloves, minced
- 2 eggplants, cut
- 2 summer squash or zucchini
- 2 tbsp of tomato paste
- ¼ cup of fresh chopped basil leaves
- 2 tomatoes, diced

Instructions

- Sautee onions.
- Mix all the veggies and add to the crockpot.
- Add chopped garlic and cooked onions to it.
- Cook at high for about four hours.

- Top with basil leaves and serve.

Nutrients: Kcal 98, Fats: 6g, Total Carbs: 11g, Proteins: 2g

14. Vegetarian Lasagna

Prep time: 20 minutes

Cook time: 2 hours

Servings: 2

Ingredients

- 2 large carrots, finely chopped
- 1/2 pound of baby bella mushrooms, roughly chopped
- 1 cup of mozzarella cheese, divided, shredded
- 1/2 tsp of salt
- 5 ounce of ricotta cheese
- 1 tbsp of olive oil
- 5 ounce can of tomato sauce
- 2 onions, finely diced
- 5-ounce jar of spaghetti sauce, divided
- 1/2 box of frozen chopped spinach, thawed & squeezed of excess moisture
- 1 tsp of Italian seasoning
- 4-5 lasagna noodles

Instructions

- Spread spaghetti sauce in the crockpot. Turn to high.
- Saute mushrooms in a pan and add salt. Once cooked, add carrots, olive oil and onions to it.
- Then add spaghetti and tomato sauce to it and remove it from the stove.
- Mix ricotta cheese, spinach, mozzarella cheese and Italian seasoning in a bowl.
- Start layering in the crockpot. Sauce is the first layer, then lasagna noodles, followed by ricotta mixture, veggie

sauce and then repeat until done.

- Cook on high for about 2 hours.
- Serve.

Nutrients: Kcal 484, Fats: 15g, Total Carbs: 53g, Proteins: 33g

15. Cheesy Brussels Sprouts

Prep time: 15 minutes

Cook time: 2 hours

Servings: 2

Ingredients

- 1 tbsp of unsalted butter
- ½ tsp of kosher salt
- 1 tbsp of heavy cream
- ½ lb of halved & trimmed Brussels sprouts
- 1 cup of Parmesan cheese, grated
- 2 cloves of garlic, sliced
- 1 oz of cream cheese, cubed
- ¼ tsp of black pepper
- 1/8 tsp of grated nutmeg

Instructions

- Add everything except cream, nutmeg and parmesan cheese to the crockpot and cook at low for about two hours.
- Once done, add cream, parmesan cheese, and nutmeg on top. Serve.

Nutrients: Kcal 159, Fats: 10g, Total Carbs: 14g, Proteins: 8g

16. Baked Ziti

Prep time: 10 minutes

Cook time: 2 hours

Servings: 2

Ingredients

- 1 jar (5 ounces) of meatless pasta sauce
- 1 can (5 ounces) of ricotta cheese,

whole-milk

- 1/4 cup of fresh basil, minced
- 1 large egg, beaten
- 1/4 cup of water
- 1 tsp of dried basil
- 1/2 tsp of red pepper flakes, crushed
- 1 cup of uncooked ziti
- 1 cup of mozzarella cheese, shredded
- Grated Parmesan cheese, optional

Instructions

- Mix ricotta cheese, basil, red pepper flakes and egg in a bowl.
- Add pasta sauce to the crockpot. Then add pasta and water to it. Lastly, pour the ricotta mixture on top. Sprinkle shredded mozzarella cheese on top.
- Cook on high for about 2 hours.
- Serve and enjoy.

Nutrients: Kcal 379, Fats: 17g, Total Carbs: 13g, Proteins: 23g

17. Crockpot Stuffed Peppers

Prep time: 15 minutes

Cook time: 3 hours

Servings: 2

Ingredients

- 1/2 cup of frozen corn
- 4 medium sweet red peppers, diced, seeds removed
- 1/2 tsp of ground cumin
- 1 can of black beans, rinsed & drained
- 1/3 cup of converted long grain rice, uncooked
- 1 small onion, chopped
- 1/2 cup of pepper jack cheese, shredded
- 3/4 cup of salsa

- 1 1/4 tsp of chili powder
- Reduced-fat sour cream, optional

Instructions

- Mix corn, beans, chili powder, salsa, cumin, salsa and cheese in a bowl. Add this into the peppers.
- Put peppers into the crockpot lined with cooking spray.
- Cook for about 3 hours and serve with sour cream.

Nutrients: Kcal 317, Fats: 10g, Total Carbs: 43g, Proteins: 15g

18. Vegan Tasty Chili

Prep time: 35 minutes

Cook time: 4 hours

Servings: 2

Ingredients

- 1 medium zucchini, chopped
- 1/2 can of kidney beans, rinsed & drained
- 1/2 can of tomato paste
- 1/2 tsp of ground cumin
- 1/2 can of black beans, rinsed & drained
- 1/2 tsp of salt
- 1/2 can of diced tomatoes, undrained
- 1/2 tbsp of cornmeal
- 1 cup of frozen corn
- 1/2 cup of water
- 1 large onion, chopped
- 1 medium sweet red pepper, chopped
- 1/2 can of chopped green chiles
- 1/2 tbsp of chili powder
- 1/2 tsp of dried oregano
- 1/2 ounce of Mexican chocolate, chopped

- 1/4 tsp of hot pepper sauce, optional

Instructions

- Mix water, cumin, pepper sauce, tomato paste, salt, chili powder and cornmeal in a small bowl.
- Add all the ingredients along with this mixture into the crockpot.
- Cook on low for about 4 hours.

Nutrients: Kcal 217, Fats: 1g, Total Carbs: 42g, Proteins: 11g

19. Vegan Mac & Cheese

Prep time: 5 minutes

Cook time: 10 minutes

Servings: 2

Ingredients

- ½ tsp of black pepper
- 1/2 lb of elbow macaroni or pasta
- 1 tsp of ground mustard
- 1 cup of milk
- 1.5 cups of water
- 1 tsp of kosher salt
- 2 cups of pumpkin puree
- 1 cup of cheddar cheese, shredded
- ¼ tsp of Worcestershire sauce

Instructions

- Add salt, pasta, pepper and Worcestershire sauce to the crockpot.

Cook for about 4 minutes.

- Add milk & pumpkin puree to the crockpot and cook till it is thick.
- Top with parsley, cheese & serve.

Nutrients: Kcal 273, Fats: 3g, Total Carbs: 18g, Proteins: 43g

20. Vegan Frittata

Prep time: 5 minutes

Cook time: 2 hours

Servings: 2

Ingredients

- 1/4 cup of chopped fresh spinach
- 2 eggs
- 1 sliced green onion
- ½ cup of cheese
- 1 tsp of Italian seasoning
- 1/2 tbsp of Parmesan cheese
- 1/4 cup of sliced cherry tomatoes
- 1 tsp of ghee
- 2 oz of sliced mushrooms

Instructions

- Sautee veggies in a pan.
- Then grease the crockpot and add veggies into it.
- Mix eggs, cheese and seasonings in a bowl.
- Pour it into the crockpot.
- Cook at high for about 2 hours.
- Serve.

Nutrients: Kcal 190, Fats: 13g, Total Carbs: 3g, Proteins: 14g

21. Eggplant Noodles

Prep time: 35 minutes

Cook time: 2 hours

Servings: 2

Ingredients

- 1/2 bell pepper, diced
- Noodles of 2 eggplants
- 4 oz of mozzarella cheese, shredded
- 1/2 diced onion
- 1/2 cup of cottage cheese
- 6 oz of pasta sauce

Instructions

- Add everything into the crockpot and cook at high for about 2 hours.
- Serve and enjoy.

Nutrients: Kcal 212, Fats: 5g, Total Carbs: 16g, Proteins: 14g

22. Vegan Quinoa

Prep time: 30 minutes

Cook time: 4 hours

Servings: 2

Ingredients

- 1 cup of drained, rinsed quinoa
- 1/2 tsp of black pepper
- 1 cup of organic broth
- 1/2 tsp of dried basil
- 1/2 can of white beans, drained, rinsed
- 1/2 cup of sliced mushrooms
- 1/2 cup of chopped broccoli florets
- 1 clove of garlic, minced
- 1/3 cup of chopped tomatoes
- 1/2 large zucchini, sliced
- 1/2 tsp of salt
- 1/2 tsp of dried oregano

- 1/2 cup of Parmesan cheese, shredded
- 1 small onion, diced

Instructions

- Add all the ingredients except cheese to a crockpot.
- Cook at high for about 4 hours.
- Top with cheese and serve.

Nutrients: Kcal 272, Fats: 6g, Total Carbs: 45g, Proteins: 14g

23. Squash Dal

Prep time: 10 minutes

Cook time: 3 hours

Servings: 2

Ingredients

- 1 tbsp of olive oil
- Cooked basmati rice
- 1 small diced yellow onion
- 1 cup of chopped spinach
- 2 cloves of garlic, minced
- 1 tsp of salt
- 1 butternut squash, cubed
- 1/2 tbsp of curry powder
- 1 cup of red lentils dry
- 1/2 tsp of turmeric
- 1 cup of coconut milk
- 1 tsp of chili powder
- ¼ tsp of pepper
- Sesame seeds & cilantro to garnish
- 1/2 cup of diced canned tomatoes

Instructions

- Add all the items to the crockpot except garnishes, rice & spinach.
- Cook at high for about 3 hours.
- Cook rice & spinach and serve with the

dal.

Nutrients: Kcal 383, Fats: 4g, Total Carbs: 72g, Proteins: 16g

24. Butternut Curry & Noodles

Prep time: 15 minutes

Cook time: 5 hours

Servings: 2

Ingredients

- 1/2 cup of Thai red curry paste
- ¼ cup of fresh basil or cilantro, roughly chopped
- 1 cup of coconut milk
- 1/2 cup of kale, shredded
- 1/2 cinnamon stick
- 1 cup of veggie broth
- 1/2 inch of ginger, grated
- 1/2 tbsp of fish sauce
- 1 lime, juiced
- 1/2 lb of egg noodles
- 1/2 tbsp of peanut butter
- 1 arils pomegranate, serve
- 2 cups of butternut squash, cubed

Instructions

- Add everything to the crockpot except cilantro and kale.
- Cook at low for about 5 hours.
- Once cooked, add kale and cilantro.
- Once its nicely cooked and thick, add broth.
- Cook noodles and serve with the curry topped with arils of pomegranate.

Nutrients: Kcal 317, Fats: 5g, Total Carbs: 55g, Proteins: 13g

25. Cauliflower & Potato Curry

Prep time: 10 minutes

Cook time: 5 hours

Servings: 2

Ingredients

- 1/2 cup of thai red curry paste
- 1/2 arils of pomegranate, to serve
- 1 can of coconut milk, canned
- ½ tsp of pepper
- 1 cup of veggie broth
- ½ tsp of cumin seeds
- 1 tbsp of soy sauce
- 1/2 large cauliflower head florets, cut
- 1/2 tbsp of molasses
- 1/2 lb of halved baby potatoes
- 1/2 stick cinnamon
- ½ tsp of kosher salt
- 1 cup of spinach
- Naan or steamed rice to serve with

Instructions

- Add everything to the crockpot except spinach.
- Cook at low for about 5 hours.
- Add spinach at the end.
- Serve curry topped with arils of pomegranate.

Nutrients: Kcal 393, Fats: 9g, Total Carbs: 65g, Proteins: 13g

26. Pineapple & Veggies Curry

Prep time: 10 minutes

Cook time: 6 hours

Servings: 2

Ingredients

- 1/2 can of coconut milk
- 1 onion, chopped
- 1.5 tbsp of curry powder
- 1/2 lb of sweet potatoes, peeled & cubed
- 1 tsp of salt
- 1 tsp of granulated garlic
- 1 tsp red pepper crushed
- 1/2 fresh pineapple, cubed
- 1 green bell pepper, cut
- 1 cup of garbanzo beans

Instructions

- Add everything to the crockpot except coconut milk. Add it at the end.
- Cook at low for about 6 hours.

Nutrients: Kcal 428, Fats: 12g, Total Carbs: 65g, Proteins: 15g

27. Quinoa Tacos

Prep time: 5 minutes

Cook time: 3 hours

Servings: 2

Ingredients

- 1/2 cup of tomatoes diced
- 1/3 cup of enchilada sauce
- 1/2 cup of quinoa
- 1.5 tbsp of taco seasoning
- 1/2 cup of black beans

- 1/2 cup of corn
- Flour or Corn tortillas
- 1/2 cup of veggie broth

Instructions

- Add everything to the crockpot except tortillas and cook at high for about 3 hours.
- Serve with tortillas and enjoy.

Nutrients: Kcal 553, Fats: 25g, Total Carbs: 63g, Proteins: 19g

28. Cauliflower Bolognese & Zucchini Noodles

Prep time: 40 minutes

Cook time: 3.5 hours

Servings: 2

Ingredients

- 1/2 tsp of dried oregano flakes
- 1 cauliflower head florets, cut
- ½ tsp of black pepper
- 1 cup of red onion, diced
- ¼ tsp pepper flakes
- 2 small garlic cloves, minced
- 1 cup of diced canned tomatoes
- 1/2 tsp of dried basil flakes
- ½ cup veggie broth
- ½ tsp of salt
- 2 cups of zucchini noodles

Instructions

- Add all ingredients into the crockpot except zucchini noodles.
- Cook at high for about 3.5 hours.
- Serve with zucchini noodles.

Nutrients: Kcal 350, Fats: 5g, Total Carbs: 22g, Proteins: 18g

29. Chili Mac & Cheese

Prep time: 15 minutes

Cook time: 4 hours

Servings: 2

Ingredients

- ½ tsp of salt
- 1 medium onion, chopped
- 1 cup of whole wheat uncooked pasta
- 1 bell pepper, chopped
- 1 cup of veggie broth
- ½ cup of canned pinto beans, drained, rinsed
- 1/2 tsp of cumin
- ½ cup of canned kidney beans, drained, rinsed
- ½ cup of crushed tomatoes
- 1/8 tsp of black pepper
- 1 cup of divided cheddar cheese
- 1 tsp of chili powder

Instructions

- Add everything to the crockpot except pasta and cheese.
- Cook at high for about 4 hours.
- Once cooked, add pasta & cheese.
- Serve and enjoy.

Nutrients: Kcal 428, Fats: 15g, Total Carbs: 64g, Proteins: 22g

30. Black Beans & Sweet Potato Quinoa

Prep time: 15 minutes

Cook time: 4 hours

Servings: 2

Ingredients

- ½ tsp of cumin
- ½ cup of fire-roasted canned tomatoes
- 1 cup of sweet potato, diced
- ½ tsp of salt
- 1/2 cup of red onions, diced
- 1/2 tsp of coriander
- 1/2 cup of bell peppers, diced
- ½ cup of raw quinoa
- ½ cup of organic canned black beans
- 1 cup of veggie broth
- 1 minced garlic clove
- 1 tsp of chili powder
- ½ tsp of paprika
- ½ tsp cayenne
- 1 tbsp of tomato paste
- ½ tsp of pepper

Instructions

- Add everything to the crockpot and cook at high for about 4 hours.

Nutrients: Kcal 183, Fats: 1g, Total Carbs: 37g, Proteins: 7g

Chapter 17: Soups & Stews

1. Buffalo Chicken Soup

Prep time: 10 minutes

Cook time: 4 hours

Servings: 2

Ingredients

- 2 cloves of garlic, minced
- 1/2 tbsp of olive oil
- 1 oz of cream cheese, cubed
- ½ large diced onion
- 2 cups of any broth
- ½ cup of diced celery
- 1/2 lb of cooked chicken, shredded
- 1 tbsp of buffalo sauce
- 1/4 cup of heavy cream

Instructions

- ○ Sauté onion & celery in a saucepan.
- ○ Add everything except cream cheese to the crockpot and cook at low for about 4 hours.
- ○ Once done, add cream cheese & cook for some minutes.
- ○ Serve hot.

Nutrients: Kcal 270, Fats: 16g, Total Carbs: 4g, Proteins: 27g

2. Chicken Fajita Soup

Prep time: 20 minutes

Cook time: 7 hours

Servings: 2

Ingredients

- 1 diced orange pepper
- ½ lb of chicken breast, cut
- 1/2 tbsp of chopped fresh cilantro
- 1 oz of chicken stock
- 2 large garlic cloves, minced
- 1 cup of tomatoes diced
- 1 medium diced onion
- 1 yellow pepper, diced
- 2 oz of thinly sliced mushrooms
- 1 tbsp of Taco Seasoning
- 1 tsp of sea salt

Instructions

- ○ Add everything to the crockpot.
- ○ Cook for 6 hours at low.
- ○ Shred chicken with a fork.
- ○ Add it back to the crockpot and cook for 1 more hour.

Nutrients: Kcal 73, Fats: 1.6g, Total Carbs: 4g, Proteins: 12g

3. Meatball Zoodle Soup

Prep time: 30 minutes

Cook time: 6 hours

Servings: 2

Ingredients

- 2 oz of beef stock
- 1/2 tsp of dried oregano
- 1 medium zucchini, spiraled
- ½ tsp powdered onion
- 1 celery, chopped

- 1 tbsp chopped fresh parsley
- ½ lb of minced beef
- 1 small diced onion
- 1 chopped carrot
- 2 cloves of garlic, minced
- 1 medium diced tomato
- ½ tsp of garlic salt
- 1 egg
- ½ tsp of sea salt
- 1/2 tsp of Italian seasoning
- ½ cup of shredded Parmesan cheese
- ½ tsp of black pepper

Instructions

- Add beef stock, carrots, celery, tomato, onion, and garlic salt to the crockpot.
- Add all the other ingredients to a large bowl and mix well. Make meatballs from it.
- Cook meatballs in a pan and cook until brown.
- Add meatballs to the crockpot and cook at low for about six hours.

Nutrients: Kcal 129, Fats: 6g, Total Carbs: 3g, Proteins: 15g

4. Beef Shanks & Cabbage Stew

Prep time: 15 minutes

Cook time: 9 hours

Servings: 2

Ingredients

- 2 smashed garlic cloves
- 1 beef shank
- ½ lb of baby carrots
- 1 cup of chicken broth
- 1 medium roughly chopped onion
- ½ tsp of freshly powdered black pepper
- 1/2 cabbage, sliced in wedges
- ½ tsp of kosher salt
- 1 cup of drained diced tomatoes
- 2 bay leaves
- 1 tbsp of coconut aminos

Instructions

- Add everything to the crockpot.
- Cook at low for around 9 hours.

Nutrients: Kcal 322, Fats: 7g, Total Carbs: 20g, Proteins: 43g

5. Green Chili & Chicken Soup

Prep time: 10 minutes

Cook time: 5 hours

Servings: 2

Ingredients

- 1 handful of fresh cilantro
- 1/2 lb of chicken breasts
- 1/2 tbsp of lime juice
- 2 garlic cloves, minced
- 1/2 tsp of Paprika
- 2 medium minced Jalapeños
- 1/2 tsp of cumin
- 1 medium diced white onion
- 1/2 tsp of dried oregano
- 1 medium diced Bell pepper
- 1/2 tsp of sea salt
- 3 oz can of green chilis, diced
- 2 cups of any broth

Toppings

- Jalapeños
- Lime juice
- Avocado

- Fresh cilantro

Instructions
- Add everything to the crockpot and cook at high for 5 hours.
- Serve with your preferred toppings.

Nutrients: Kcal 173, Fats: 3g, Total Carbs: 6g, Proteins: 26g

6. Jalapeno Popper Soup

Prep time: 5 minutes

Cook time: 6 hours

Servings: 2

Ingredients
- ½ lb of chicken breasts, boneless, skinless
- 1/4 cup of cheddar cheese
- 1 1/2 tbsp of butter
- ½ tsp of pepper
- 2 minced garlic cloves
- ½ tsp of cumin
- ½ chopped onion
- ½ chopped green pepper
- 2 oz of softened cream cheese
- 1 1/2 cups of chicken broth
- 1 chopped seeded jalapeno
- ¼ tsp of paprika
- ½ lb of crumbled cooked bacon
- ½ cup of heavy cream
- 1/2 tsp of salt
- 1/4 cup of Monterrey cheese
- ½ tsp of xanthan gum

Instructions
- Saute onions, green peppers and jalapenos in a saucepan. Also add seasonings.
- Then add this veggie mixture and chicken breasts to the crockpot.
- Cook at low for 6 hours.
- Once chicken is out, take it out, shred and put it back.
- Add cream cheese, whipping cream and prepared bacon stirring to the crockpot.
- Cook for 10 more minutes.
- Add xanthan gum and cook for 15 more minutes.
- Add bacon and cheddar cheese on top & serve.

Nutrients: Kcal 571, Fats: 40g, Total Carbs: 2g, Proteins: 40g

7. Crockpot Taco Soup

Prep time: 10 minutes

Cook time: 2 hours

Servings: 2

Ingredients
- 2 cups of beef broth
- 1/2 lb of minced beef, cooked
- ½ tsp of chili powder
- 1 tbsp of minced garlic
- 1 cup of cream cheese
- 1 tbsp of taco seasoning
- ½ cup of diced canned green chilis
- 2 cups of onion
- 1 cup of diced tomatoes

Instructions
- Add everything to the crockpot.
- Cook at high for about 2 hours.

Nutrients: Kcal 369, Fats: 24g, Total Carbs: 6g, Proteins: 30g

8. Roasted Cauliflower & White Cheddar Soup

Prep time: 30 minutes

Cook time: 3 hours

Servings: 2

Ingredients

- 2 chopped garlic cloves
- 1/2 small cauliflower head, cut
- ½ tsp of salt & pepper
- 1 tbsp of olive oil
- 1 cup of shredded aged cheddar
- 1 onion, diced
- 1 cup of chicken stock
- 1 cup of milk
- ½ tsp of scallions

Instructions

- Preheat oven to 400 degrees F. Season cauliflower with salt & pepper. Add some oil and bake in oven until golden.
- Saute onions in a pan. Add thyme and garlic to it.
- Add everything to the crockpot except milk and cheese.
- Cook at high for 2 hours.
- Then add milk and cheese. Cook for some more minutes and then serve.

Nutrients: Kcal 384, Fats: 28g, Total Carbs: 12g, Proteins: 17g

9. Zuppa Toscana Soup

Prep time: 10 minutes

Cook time: 4 hours

Servings: 2

Ingredients

- 1/2 lb of minced Italian sausage
- ½ tsp of pepper
- 1 tbsp of oil
- ¼ tsp crushed pepper flakes
- ½ cup of onions, finely diced
- ½ lb of chicken
- 1 1/2 cups of kale, chopped
- 2 cloves of garlic, minced
- 1/2 tsp of salt
- ½ cup of heavy cream

Instructions

- Brown ground sausage in a pan.
- Saute onions in a pan.
- Add everything except heavy cream to the crockpot.
- Cook at high for 4 hours.
- Once done. Add heavy cream, mix and serve.

Nutrients: Kcal 215, Fats: 16g, Total Carbs: 6g, Proteins: 10g

10. Crockpot Chicken Stew

Prep time: 5 minutes

Cook time: 2 hours

Servings: 2

Ingredients

- 1 cup of chicken stock
- ½ tsp of salt & pepper
- 1 medium finely diced carrot
- 1/2 cup of fresh spinach
- 1 diced celery stick
- ¼ tsp of dried thyme
- ½ cup of diced onion
- 10 oz of chicken thighs boneless, cubed in 1" pieces
- 2 minced garlic cloves
- 1/2 fresh rosemary spring

- ½ tsp of dried oregano
- ½ cup of heavy cream
- xanthan gum, to thicken

Instructions

- Add everything except salt, spinach, heavy cream, xanthan gum and pepper to the crockpot.
- Cook at high for 2 hours.
- Add the leftover ingredients and cook for 10 minutes.

Nutrients: Kcal 228, Fats: 11g, Total Carbs: 6g, Proteins: 23g

11. Turkey Kale Rice Soup

Prep time: 15 minutes

Cook time: 8 hours

Servings: 2

Ingredients

- 1 tbsp of olive oil
- 1 cup of miracle rice
- ½ cup of chopped shallots
- ½ tsp of dried basil
- 2 cups of broth
- 1 minced garlic clove
- ½ cup of sliced carrots
- ½ tsp of dried thyme
- 1/2 tsp of salt
- ½ tsp of dried oregano
- 1 cup of chopped turkey, cooked
- ½ tsp of pepper
- 2 cups of water
- 1 cup of sliced celery
- 2 cups of chopped kale

Instructions

- Saute veggies in a pan.

- Add salt, oregano, thyme, basil and pepper into it. Cook for a while.
- Mix all ingredients except the rice.
- Cook at high for 3 hours.
- Add rice to crockpot in the last 30 minutes of cooking.

Nutrients: Kcal 81, Fats: 4g, Total Carbs: 5g, Proteins: 8g

12. Andouille Sausage & Cabbage Soup

Prep time: 15 minutes

Cook time: 4 hours

Servings: 2

Ingredients

- 5 oz of andouille sliced sausage
- 1/2 tsp of caraway seeds
- ½ tbsp of EVOO
- ½ cup of chopped shallots
- 1/2 tsp of celery salt
- 2 cloves minced garlic
- 2 cups of chicken broth
- 2 cups of thinly sliced cabbage
- 1 cup of chopped carrots
- 2 cups of water
- 1/2 tsp of onion powder
- ½ tsp of dried thyme
- 1/2 tsp of fennel seeds
- 1/2 tbsp of apple vinegar

Instructions

- Saute sausage, garlic and shallots in a pan.
- Add everything to the crockpot.
- Cook at high for 4 hours.

Nutrients: Kcal 132, Fats: 9g, Total Carbs: 4g, Proteins: 6g

13. Cabbage Roll Soup

Prep time: 20 minutes

Cook time: 3 hours

Servings: 2

Ingredients

- 1 tbsp of EVOO
- 2 cups of low sodium beef broth
- 1 minced garlic clove
- 1 tbsp of marinara sauce
- ½ cup of chopped onion
- 1/2 tsp of pepper
- ½ cup of chopped shallots
- 1/2 lb of minced beef
- 1/2 tsp of parsley, dried
- 1/2 tsp of salt
- 1 cup of riced cauliflower
- ½ tsp of oregano, dried
- 2 cups of sliced cabbage

Instructions

- Saute onion, garlic and shallots in a pan.
- Then add ground beef to it and let it cook. Once brown, add marinara sauce and seasonings to it.
- Add everything to the crockpot.
- Cook at high for 3 hours.

Nutrients: Kcal 356, Fats: 26g, Total Carbs: 6g, Proteins: 20g

14. Tasty Chicken Taco Soup

Prep time: 10 minutes

Cook time: 4 hours

Servings: 2

Ingredients

- 1/2 lb of chicken breasts
- ¼ tsp of salt
- 2 cups of chicken broth
- 1 tsp of chili powder
- 1 cup of Rotel canned tomatoes
- ½ tsp of cumin
- 1 cup of cream cheese
- ½ cup of diced onion
- 1 tsp of paprika
- 2 minced garlic cloves
- 1 tbsp of lemon juice

Instructions

- Add everything to the crockpot.
- Cook on a high setting for 4 hours.

Nutrients: Kcal 360, Fats: 23g, Total Carbs: 7g, Proteins: 30g

15. Chicken Noodle Soup

Prep time: 15 minutes

Cook time: 3 hours

Servings: 2

Ingredients

- 1 tsp of fresh ginger root, minced
- 1/2 lb boneless skinless, cubed chicken breasts
- 1 cup of halved snow peas, fresh
- 2 medium shredded carrots
- 1 1/2 tbsp of chicken broth reduced-sodium
- 3 cups of chicken broth reduced-sodium
- 1 tbsp of rice vinegar
- 1/2 tbsp of soy sauce reduced-sodium
- 1/4 tsp of pepper
- 1 cup of water
- 1 oz of angel hair uncooked pasta

Instructions

- Add everything except pasta and peas to the crockpot.
- Cook at low for 4 hours.
- Add peas & pasta and cook for 30 more minutes.

Nutrients: Kcal 126, Fats: 2g, Total Carbs: 7g, Proteins: 16g

16. Black Bean Soup

Prep time: 5 minutes

Cook time: 4 hours

Servings: 2

Ingredients

- 4 oz can of drained rinsed black beans
- 1/2 tsp of powdered cumin
- 4 oz can of stewed tomatoes
- 2 thinly sliced green onions
- 4 oz can of diced tomatoes
- 2 oz of green chilis, chopped
- 4 oz can of chicken broth
- 1 tsp of chili powder
- 4 oz of drained Mexicorn
- 1/2 tsp of minced garlic

Instructions

- Add everything to the crockpot.
- Cook at high for 4 hours.

Nutrients: Kcal 91, Fats: 0g, Total Carbs: 9g, Proteins: 4g

17. Broccoli Cheddar Soup

Prep time: 20 minutes

Cook time: 4 hours

Servings: 2

Ingredients

- 1/2 lb of broccoli florets, frozen

- 1 cup of cheddar cheese, shredded
- 2 cups of chicken broth low-sodium
- 1/8 tsp of cayenne pepper
- 1/2 tsp of freshly powdered black pepper
- 1 medium diced onion
- 1/4 tsp of seasoned salt
- 2 medium finely diced carrots
- 1 1/2 lbs. melting cheese
- 5 oz of celery soup cream cans
- 1/4 tsp of kosher salt
- Crackers to serve

Instructions

- Add everything except cheese and crackers to the crockpot.
- Cook at high for 4 hours.
- Puree it using a processor.
- Add it back to the crockpot, mix cheese in it, cook for 15 minutes at low.
- Serve with crackers.

Nutrients: Kcal 302, Fats: 21g, Total Carbs: 12g, Proteins: 17g

18. Green Soup

Prep Time: 10 minutes

Cook Time: 3 hours

Servings: 2

Ingredients

- 2 cups of vegetable broth low-sodium
- 1 tbsp of fresh lemon juice
- 1 cup of diced unpeeled potatoes
- 2 stems of Swiss chard, thinly sliced
- 1 cup of florets of cauliflower
- 1/2 tsp of freshly powdered black pepper
- 1 cup of florets of broccoli

- 1/2 tsp of kosher salt
- 1 small diced yellow onion
- 1 tbsp olive oil
- 1/8 tsp of pepper flakes
- 4 oz of frozen peas
- 2 cloves of garlic, minced
- 1/2 tsp of fresh dill chopped

Instructions

- Add everything except chard stems, peas, leaves, lemon juice and dill to the crockpot.
- Cook at low for 3 hours.
- Add chard stems and cook at low for 5 minutes.
- Then add peas, dill, chard leaves and lemon juice to it. Cook for 3 minutes.
- Serve.

Nutrients: Kcal 50, Fats: 2g, Total Carbs: 7g, Proteins: 1g

19. Mexican Soup

Prep time: 15 minutes

Cook time: 4 hours

Servings: 2

Ingredients

- 3 cups of water
- 1/2 lb of chicken giblets removed
- 2 sliced carrots
- 1 tsp dried mint
- 2 chopped garlic cloves
- 1 sliced stemmed jalapeño
- 1 coarsely chopped large onion
- 2 sliced celery stalks
- 1 tsp kosher salt
- 1/2 tsp dried marjoram
- 2 dry bay leaves

- 1/2 cilantro bunch
- 1 quartered lime

Instructions

- Add everything to the crockpot.
- Cook at high for 4 hours.
- Remove chicken bones and shred it. Add it back to the crockpot.
- Cook for 5 more minutes and then serve.

Nutrients: Kcal 444, Fats: 23g, Total Carbs: 16g, Proteins: 36g

20. Mediterranean Beef Stew

Prep time: 20 minutes

Cook time: 8 hours

Servings: 2

Ingredients

- 1 tbsp of olive oil
- 1 tsp of salt
- 1 cup of sliced mushrooms
- 1 tsp of capers
- 1 small onion, diced
- 1 tsp of pepper
- 1 lb of chuck steak, trimmed & diced
- 1 tsp of rosemary, chopped
- 1 cup of beef stock
- ½ can of diced tomatoes with juice
- ¼ cup of balsamic vinegar
- ½ cup of tomato sauce
- 3 garlic cloves, thinly sliced
- 1 tsp of parsley, chopped
- 1/2 can of black olives

Instructions

- Saute mushrooms in a pan until brown.

- Cook beef until brown.
- Add everything to the crockpot.
- Cook at low for 8 hours.

Nutrients: Kcal 540, Fats: 32g, Total Carbs: 10g, Proteins: 46g

21. Apple Chicken Stew

Prep time: 35 minutes

Cook time: 3 hours

Servings: 2

Ingredients

- 1/2 lb potatoes
- 1 sliced celery rib
- 1/4 tsp dried thyme
- 1 lb chicken breasts
- 1/2 tbsp cider vinegar
- ½ tsp pepper
- 1 tbsp olive oil
- ½ tsp caraway seeds
- 1/2 tsp salt
- 2 carrots, cut
- 1 bay leaf
- 1 cubed apple
- 1 sliced red onion
- 1 cup apple juice
- 1/2 tsp parsley

Instructions1

- Add everything to the crockpot
- Cook at high for 3 hours.

Nutrients: Kcal 284, Fats: 6g, Total Carbs: 20g, Proteins: 26g

22. Bacon Cabbage Stew

Prep time: 10 minutes

Cook time: 7 hours

Servings: 2

Ingredients

- 1 tsp of black pepper
- ½ lb of organic bacon, cut into strips
- 1/2 tsp of thyme
- 1 lb of grass-fed chuck roast
- 1 tsp of sea salt
- 1 red onion
- 1 garlic clove, smashed
- 1 cup of beef bone broth
- 1/2 green cabbage

Instructions

- Add everything to the crockpot.
- Cook for 7 hours at low.

Nutrients: Kcal 272, Fats: 20g, Total Carbs: 8g, Proteins: 15g

23. Lamb Stew

Prep time: 20 minutes

Cook time: 2 hours

Servings: 2

Ingredients

- 1/4 cup of rosemary leaves
- 1/2 cup of tallow
- 1 lb lamb shoulder with the bone in
- 2 crushed garlic cloves
- 1/2 cup of tomato puree
- 1 large diced onion
- 1 tsp pepper
- 2 celery sticks
- 1 tsp salt

- 1/2 cup wine vinegar
- 2 cups of beef stock
- 1/2 lb mushrooms sliced

Instructions

- Cook herbs, spices, stock and lamb in a pan.
- Then add it to the crockpot.
- Cook at high for about 2 hours.
- Cook the herbs and spices together in a pan for about five minutes.
- Serve with cheese or any sauce.

Nutrients: Kcal 462, Fats: 37g, Total Carbs: 2g, Proteins: 30g

24. Pork Stew

Prep time: 15 minutes

Cook time: 5 hours

Servings: 2

Ingredients

- 1 tenderloin of pork
- 1 rosemary sprig
- 1/2 tsp salt
- 4 minced garlic cloves
- ½ tsp pepper
- 2 tbsp tomato paste
- 2 carrots chopped
- 3 cups of beef broth
- 2 chopped celery ribs
- 2 fresh bay leaves
- 1 medium chopped onion
- 1/3 cup dried plums
- 1 thyme sprig

Instructions

- Add all ingredients to the crockpot.
- Cook at low for 5 hours.

- Serve.

Nutrients: Kcal 177, Fats: 4g, Total Carbs: 9g, Proteins: 24g

25. Fish Stew

Prep time: 5 minutes

Cook time: 6 hours

Servings: 2

Ingredients

- 2 tbsp EVOO
- 1 tbsp lemon juice
- 1 medium sliced red onion
- ½ tsp of red pepper crushed
- 2 chopped garlic cloves
- ½ tsp of black pepper
- ½ cup white wine dry
- 1 tbsp fresh chopped dill
- 2 oz clam juice
- ½ tsp of kosher salt
- ½ lb diced potatoes
- 2 cups of water
- 5 oz tomatoes diced
- 1 lb sea bass

Instructions

- Put everything in crockpot except dill, fish, lemon juice, and oil.
- Cook at low for 6 hours.
- Add all the leftover ingredients.
- Cook for some more minutes. Serve.

Nutrients: Kcal 471, Fats: 20g, Total Carbs: 24g, Proteins: 43g

26. Moroccan Chickpea Stew

Prep time: 10 minutes

Cook time: 4 hours

Servings: 2

Ingredients

- 1 medium chopped white onion
- 1/2 tsp pepper
- 2 minced garlic cloves
- 1/2 tsp cinnamon
- 1 small chopped butternut squash
- 1 tsp turmeric
- 1 chopped bell pepper
- 2 cups veggie broth
- 1/4 cup of red lentils
- 1 tsp grated ginger
- 5 oz rinsed, drained canned chickpeas
- 1 tsp smoked paprika
- 5 oz pure canned tomato sauce
- 1 tsp cumin
- 1/2 tsp salt

Instructions

- Add everything to the crockpot.
- Cook at high for 4 hours.

Nutrients: Kcal 178, Fats: 0g, Total Carbs: 37g, Proteins: 8g

27. Vegan White Bean Stew

Prep time: 20 minutes

Cook time: 4 hours

Servings: 2

Ingredients

- 1 lb white beans
- 2 cups of chopped kale, chard & spinach
- 1 large diced carrot
- 1/2 tsp black pepper
- 1 large diced celery stalk
- 1/2 tsp oregano
- 1 diced onion
- 1/2 tsp rosemary
- 2 garlic cloves chopped
- 1 bay leaf
- 1/2 tsp thyme
- 3 cups water
- 1/2 tsp of salt
- 2 oz diced tomatoes
- Rice, or bread to serve

Instructions

- Add everything except tomatoes, chopped greens and seasonings to the crockpot.
- Cook at high for 4 hours.
- Add all the other ingredients and cook at high for 1.5 hours.
- Serve with rice or bread.

Nutrients: Kcal 316, Fats: 8g, Total Carbs: 43g, Proteins: 18g

28. Curried Vegetable & Chickpea Stew

Prep time: 30 minutes

Cook time: 4 hours

Servings: 2

Ingredients

- 1 tsp olive oil
- 2 oz baby spinach
- 1 large diced onion
- 4 canned tomatoes, diced
- 2 garlic cloves minced

- 1 tsp kosher salt
- ½ cauliflower head florets
- 1 medium diced potato
- 1 tsp curry powder
- 4 oz of chickpeas canned
- 1 tsp packed brown sugar
- 1 cup of vegetable broth
- 1 tsp grated ginger
- 2 medium diced bell pepper
- ¼ tsp black pepper
- 1 cup of coconut milk

Instructions

- Sauté onion & potato in a pan. Then add cayenne, brown sugar, garlic, broth and curry powder to it. Cook for some time.
- Add everything except spinach and coconut milk to the crockpot.
- Cook at high for 4 hours.
- Add coconut milk and spinach at the end and cook for some minutes.
- Serve.

Nutrients: Kcal 255, Fats: 9g, Total Carbs: 38g, Proteins: 10g

29. Shrimp Stew

Prep time: 5 minutes

Cook time: 1 hour

Servings: 2

Ingredients

- ½ lb of raw shrimps
- 1 tbsp of fresh lime juice
- ¼ cup of olive oil
- ½ cup of coconut milk
- 1 onion, diced
- ¼ cup of fresh cilantro, chopped

- 1 clove of garlic, minced
- 1 can of diced tomatoes w/ chilies
- 1 tbsp of sriracha hot sauce
- 1 tsp of roasted red pepper, diced
- Salt & pepper, to taste

Instructions

- Saute onions in a pan. Then add peppers and garlic to it. Cook until brown.
- Add everything to the crockpot except coconut milk, Cook at high for an hour.
- Add coconut milk at the end.
- Serve,

Nutrients: Kcal 294, Fats: 19g, Total Carbs: 5g, Proteins: 24g

30. Creamy Cauliflower Soup

Prep time: 5 minutes

Cook time: 1 hour

Servings: 2

Ingredients

- 1 tbsp of salted butter
- 1 cup of milk
- 1 tbsp of olive oil
- 2 tsp of cornstarch
- 1/3 cauliflower, cut into small florets
- ½ tsp of thyme
- 1 onion, diced
- 1 stalk of celery, sliced
- 2 garlic cloves, minced
- 1 carrot, diced
- ½ tsp of dried oregano
- 1 cup of vegetable broth
- Salt and pepper to taste

Instructions

- Cook all the veggies in a pan.
- Add everything to the crockpot.
- Cook at low for an hour.
- Serve hot.

Nutrients: Kcal 149, Fats: 8g, Total Carbs: 14g, Proteins: 3g

31. Chicken Tortellini Soup

Prep time: 10 minutes

Cook time: 4 hours 10 minutes

Servings: 2

Ingredients

- 1 onion, diced
- 3 cups chicken broth
- 3 medium carrots peeled, halved & sliced
- 1/2 tsp of dried thyme
- 3 stalks of celery, sliced
- 3/4 tsp of salt
- 1 lb of boneless skinless chicken breasts
- 1/2 tsp of pepper
- 1 tsp of dried parsley
- 1 tsp of minced garlic
- 1 pack of cheese tortellini

Instructions

- Add everything except tortellini to the crockpot.
- Cook at high for 4 hours.
- Take out the chicken, shred it using a fork and put it back to the crockpot.
- Add tortellini to it and cook for 10 more minutes.
- Serve.

Nutrients: Kcal 380, Fats: 9g, Total Carbs:

37g, Proteins: 36g

32. Chicken & Wild Rice Soup

Prep time: 20 minutes

Cook time: 30 minutes

Servings: 2

Ingredients

- 2 slices of bacon, chopped
- salt and pepper to taste
- 1/2 tsp of minced garlic
- 1/2 onion, diced
- 1 1/2 cups of cooked wild rice
- 1 carrot peeled, halved & sliced
- 2 1/2 cups of chicken broth
- 1 stalk of celery, thinly sliced
- ½ cup of flour
- 1 cup of cooked shredded chicken
- ½ cup of heavy cream
- 1 tbsp of chopped fresh parsley

Instructions

- Cook bacon in a pan until browned.
- Add celery, bacon, carrots and onions to the pot. Cook for 6 minutes. Then add salt, garlic and pepper. Cook for about 30 seconds.
- Add all the other ingredients to the pot and cook at low for 25 minutes.
- Serve.

Nutrients: Kcal 408, Fats: 20g, Total Carbs: 29g, Proteins: 24g

33. Chicken Gnocchi Soup

Prep time: 20 minutes

Cook time: 1 hour

Servings: 2

Ingredients

- 1 tbsp of butter
- ½ tsp of chopped parsley
- 1/3 cup of onion, chopped
- 1/2 cup of baby spinach leaves
- ½ cup of celery, sliced
- 1 tbsp of all-purpose flour
- 5 ounces gnocchi
- 1 tsp of minced garlic
- 1/2 cup of shredded carrots
- salt and pepper to taste
- 1 cup of cooked chicken, cut into 3/4-inch pieces
- 1 tsp of Italian seasoning
- 1 cup of chicken broth

Instructions

- Add celery, butter, salt, pepper and onions to the pan. Cook well.
- Add everything to the crockpot and cook for an hour.
- Serve and enjoy.

Nutrients: Kcal 318, Fats: 16g, Total Carbs: 39g, Proteins: 7g

34. Chicken Enchilada Soup

Prep time: 20 minutes

Cook time: 1 hour

Servings: 2

Ingredients

- 1 tsp of olive oil
- 1 tbsp of cilantro, chopped
- 1/2 cup corn kernels frozen, fresh or canned
- 1/2 cup of onion diced
- 7.25 ounce can of diced tomatoes
- ½ tsp of garlic minced
- 5 ounce can of red enchilada sauce
- 1/2 cup of corn flour
- 1/2 cup shredded cheddar cheese
- 2 cups of chicken broth
- 7.5 ounce can of black beans, drained & rinsed
- 2 ounce can of diced green chiles
- 1 cup of cooked chicken, shredded
- salt and pepper to taste

Instructions

- Add everything to the crockpot.
- Cook at high for an hour.

Nutrients: Kcal 418, Fats: 17g, Total Carbs: 33g, Proteins: 37g

35. Ham Bone Soup

Prep time: 10 minutes

Cook time: 4 hours

Servings: 2

Ingredients

- 1 yellow onion, peeled & chopped
- 1/3 cup of chopped parsley
- 1 carrot peeled, quartered & sliced
- 1 cup of diced ham
- 1 ham bone
- 1 tsp of dried thyme
- 1 20-ounce bag of dried bean soup mix
- 1 tsp of minced garlic
- 1/2 15 ounce can of diced tomatoes undrained

- 2 ½ cups of low sodium chicken broth
- salt and pepper to taste

Instructions

- Add everything to the crockpot.
- Cook at high for 4 hours.
- Remove the ham bone.
- Top with some parsley and serve.

Nutrients: Kcal 412, Fats: 5g, Total Carbs: 67g, Proteins: 38g

36. Bean & Ham Soup

Prep time: 10 minutes

Cook time: 4 hours 20 minutes

Servings: 2

Ingredients

- 6 ounce bag of dried bean soup mix
- salt and pepper to taste
- 1/3 cup of onion finely diced
- 5 ounce can of diced tomatoes, undrained
- 1 sprig of fresh thyme
- 1 carrot peeled, halved & sliced
- 1 cup of diced ham
- ½ stalk of celery, sliced
- 1/2 bay leaf
- 2 1/2 cups of low sodium chicken broth
- 1/3 tsp of minced garlic
- 1/4 cup of chopped fresh parsley

Instructions

- Add everything to the crockpot.
- Cook at high for 4 hours & 20 minutes.
- Top with some parsley and serve.

Nutrients: Kcal 462, Fats: 5g, Total Carbs: 70g, Proteins: 38g

37. Baked Potato Soup

Prep time: 10 minutes

Cook time: 6 hours

Servings: 2

Ingredients

- 1/2 lb of potatoes, diced
- 2 garlic cloves, minced
- ¼ tsp of salt
- 1/2 cup of cream cheese
- 2 cups of chicken broth
- 1 small onion, diced
- ¼ tsp of black pepper

Instructions

- Add everything to the crockpot except cream cheese.
- Cook at low for 6 hours.
- Add cream cheese at the end.
- Cook for some minutes and serve.

Nutrients: Kcal 342, Fats: 5g, Total Carbs: 34g, Proteins: 23g

38. Stuffed Pepper Soup

Prep time: 10 minutes

Cook time: 6 hours

Servings: 2

Ingredients

- 3 cups of beef broth
- 1/2 lb of ground beef
- 1 tbsp of brown sugar
- 2 green bell peppers, diced
- 1 cup of water
- ½ can of diced tomatoes, undrained
- 2 cloves of garlic, minced
- 1/3 can of tomato sauce
- 1 small onion, diced

Instructions

- Add everything to the crockpot.
- Cook at low for 6 hours.
- Serve.

Nutrients: Kcal 446, Fats: 25g, Total Carbs: 64g, Proteins: 33g

39. Spinach Soup

Prep time: 10 minutes

Cook time: 5 hours

Servings: 2

Ingredients

- 2 cloves of garlic, minced
- 2 cups of chicken broth
- 1 tsp of salt
- 2 cups of spinach, cut
- 1 cup of water
- 1 tsp of black pepper
- 1 small onion, diced

Instructions

- Add everything to the crockpot.
- Cook at low for 5 hours.

Nutrients: Kcal 246, Fats: 11g, Total Carbs: 34g, Proteins: 23g

40. Kale Soup

Prep time: 10 minutes

Cook time: 4 hours

Servings: 2

Ingredients

- 2 cloves of garlic, minced
- 2 cups of chicken broth
- 1 tsp of salt
- 2 cups of kale, diced
- 1 cup of water
- 1 tsp of red chili flakes

- ½ tsp of oregano
- 1 tsp of black pepper
- ½ tsp of thyme

Instructions

- Add everything to the crockpot.
- Cook at low for 4 hours.
- Serve hot and enjoy.

Nutrients: Kcal 146, Fats: 5g, Total Carbs: 24g, Proteins: 13g

41. Tasty Butternut Soup

Prep time: 15 minutes

Cook time: 6 hours

Servings: 2

Ingredients

- 2 cloves of garlic, minced
- ½ tsp of red chili flakes
- ½ tsp of ginger, minced
- 2 cups of chicken broth
- 1 tsp of salt
- 2 cups of butternut, diced
- 1 cup of water
- ½ tbsp of cream
- ½ tsp of oregano
- 1 tsp of black pepper
- ½ tsp of thyme

Instructions

- Add everything to the crockpot.
- Cook at low for 6 hours.
- Serve hot.

Nutrients: Kcal 231, Fats: 7g, Total Carbs: 31g, Proteins: 15g

42. Rice & Red Beans Soup

Prep time: 30 minutes

Cook time: 8 hours

Servings: 2

Ingredients

- 1 chopped onion
- 2 dry bay leaves
- 1 tsp of olive oil
- ½ tbsp of Worcestershire sauce
- 1 tsp of garlic, finely minced
- 3 sausages
- 1/2 tsp of thyme, dried
- 1/2 tsp of any spicy seasoning
- 1 cup of white rice, cooked
- 1 cup of red beans
- 2 cups of chicken stock
- 1/2 tsp of oregano, dried
- 1/2 tsp of Tabasco Sauce

Instructions

- Saute onion in a pan.
- Brown sausages in a pan until brown.
- Add everything to the crockpot.
- Cook at low for 8 hours.
- Serve hot.

Nutrients: Kcal 671, Fats: 36g, Total Carbs: 24g, Proteins: 29g

43. Greek Soup

Prep time: 30 minutes

Cook time: 8 hours

Servings: 2

Ingredients

- 1 cup of cooked diced chicken
- 3 cups of chicken broth
- ½ cup of garbanzo beans
- 1 tsp of Greek seasoning
- 1 tsp of fresh oregano
- 1 small diced onion
- 1 tsp of garlic minced
- 1 tsp of the base of vegetable soup
- ½ cup of diced petite tomatoes
- 1/2 tsp of fresh parsley, chopped

Instructions

- Add everything to the crockpot.
- Cook at low for 8 hours.

Nutrients: Kcal 321, Fats: 17g, Total Carbs: 32g, Proteins: 25g

44. Cabbage & Ham Soup

Prep time: 30 minutes

Cook time: 7 hours

Servings: 2

Ingredients

- 1/2 head of cabbage, cut
- 2 cups of chicken stock
- 1 tsp of Spike Seasoning
- 1/2 cup of onion, chopped
- 1 finely chopped bell pepper
- 1 dry bay leaf
- 2 small chopped carrots
- 1 tsp of crushed garlic
- 1 cup of lean ham, diced
- 1 tsp of any seasoning
- 1 tsp of coarse crushed black pepper
- 1 tsp of dried parsley
- 1 cup of water

Instructions

- Add everything to the crockpot.

- Cook at low for 7 hours.
- Serve and enjoy.

Nutrients: Kcal 241, Fats: 7g, Total Carbs: 8g, Proteins: 25g

45. Bean & Cabbage Soup

Prep time: 15 minutes

Cook time: 10 hours

Servings: 2

Ingredients

- 1 tsp of powdered onion
- 1/2 cup of Anasazi Beans, dried
- 1/2 cup of diced ham
- 2 dry bay leaves
- 1/2 cup of cabbage, finely chopped
- 1/2 cup of celery, diced
- 1 tsp of powdered garlic
- 1/2 cup of carrots, diced
- 2 cups of water
- 1/2 cup of onion, diced
- 1 tsp of parsley, dried
- ½ tsp of freshly powdered black pepper

Instructions

- Add everything to the crockpot.
- Cook at low for 10 hours.
- Serve hot.

Nutrients: Kcal 91, Fats: 1g, Total Carbs: 20g, Proteins: 5g

46. Pumpkin Soup

Prep time: 10 minutes

Cook time: 8 hours

Servings: 2

Ingredients

- 1 cup of chopped fresh pumpkin
- 1 tsp of canola oil
- 2 cups of chicken broth
- 1/2 tsp of salt
- 2 small chopped tart apples
- 1 tsp of fresh minced ginger root
- 1 medium chopped onion
- 1 minced garlic clove
- 1 tsp of lemon juice
- 1/4 cup of pumpkin seeds

Instructions

- Add everything to the crockpot.
- Cook at low for 8 hours.
- Serve & enjoy.

Nutrients: Kcal 102, Fats: 2g, Total Carbs: 18g, Proteins: 3g

COOKING CONVERSION CHART

Measurement

CUP	ONCES	MILLILITERS	TABLESPOONS
8 cup	64 oz	1895 ml	128
6 cup	48 oz	1420 ml	96
5 cup	40 oz	1180 ml	80
4 cup	32 oz	960 ml	64
2 cup	16 oz	480 ml	32
1 cup	8 oz	240 ml	16
3/4 cup	6 oz	177 ml	12
2/3 cup	5 oz	158 ml	11
1/2 cup	4 oz	118 ml	8
3/8 cup	3 oz	90 ml	6
1/3 cup	2.5 oz	79 ml	5.5
1/4 cup	2 oz	59 ml	4
1/8 cup	1 oz	30 ml	3
1/16 cup	1/2 oz	15 ml	1

Temperature

FAHRENHEIT	CELSIUS
100 °F	37 °C
150 °F	65 °C
200 °F	93 °C
250 °F	121 °C
300 °F	150 °C
325 °F	160 °C
350 °F	180 °C
375 °F	190 °C
400 °F	200 °C
425 °F	220 °C
450 °F	230 °C
500 °F	260 °C
525 °F	274 °C
550 °F	288 °C

Weight

IMPERIAL	METRIC
1/2 oz	15 g
1 oz	29 g
2 oz	57 g
3 oz	85 g
4 oz	113 g
5 oz	141 g
6 oz	170 g
8 oz	227 g
10 oz	283 g
12 oz	340 g
13 oz	369 g
14 oz	397 g
15 oz	425 g
1 lb	453 g

Chapter 18: Bonus Chapter

18.1 How to Cook Rice in a Crockpot?

Rice is one of the meals that may be prepared in various ways. There is no limit to the variety of seasonings that may be used. Rice cooked in a crockpot is so simple to prepare that it is almost impossible to mess up. After adding some water and rice to the pot, you can step back and let it do the work. With very little work on your part, you will get rice that is fluffy, flavorful, and precisely cooked.

You will need the following items to create this easy recipe:

- Rice
- Salt
- Water
- Cooking spray, nonstick

When preparing rice in a crockpot, put it in a strainer and run it under cold water first. Place the strainer in the sink. This assists in removing some of the additional starch that is present on the surface of the rice. If you do this step, you will end up with rice that is correctly cooked and soft since it will assist in minimizing clumping. The essential step is maintaining the rinsing until the water becomes completely clear.

Next, spray your crockpot with nonstick cooking spray to prevent food from sticking. After that, put some rice, water, and a little salt. Cook, covered, on high for about two and a half hours. After the consistency has been achieved to your satisfaction, serve and enjoy.

When preparing rice in this manner, it is recommended that a considerable quantity of rice be prepared. Remember that you will need one cup of rice for every two cups of water. This is the most important thing to keep in mind. In this manner, for instance, if you wanted to boil two cups of rice, you would want about four cups of water, yielding 6 cups of cooked rice.

18.2 Tips &Tricks for Cooking Chicken in the Crockpot

It doesn't matter what sort of chicken supper you have planned for your crockpot; you can be sure that it will be simple to prepare and quite tasty. And to make it even more enjoyable, here are some suggestions for you to use.

- Preheating your crockpot is essential at any time, but it is particularly crucial when adding chicken that has been browned on the outside or aromatics that have been sautéed, as is the case with chicken curry. When you put hot items into a cold crockpot, everything needs to heat back up again, which may add 10 to 20 minutes to the total amount of time it takes to cook the dish.

- Chicken meals made in a crockpot are easiest to prepare on the weekends, during meal prep time, or any other period that allows you to get a head start on the evening meal. Chicken needs to lend itself better to recipes that call for an all-day cook period.

- If preparing chicken in a crockpot, check the time closely or set a timer for yourself. The preparation time for many dishes is no more than a few hours. Even when using a crockpot, chicken cooked excessively can lose its appealing moist bite and become somewhat dry.

- Before adding chicken to a crockpot, it is best to sear it in a hot pan on the stovetop. There are very few situations in which this step is optional, but two that immediately spring to mind are shredding the chicken and poaching it. The deep sear not only gives the meat an outstanding color but also adds a richer taste that cannot be achieved with the crockpot.

- The chicken flesh in any recipe that calls for a crockpot will, throughout cooking, absorb the flavors of any other ingredients that are added to the dish. Because of this, if a supper calls for a sauce or even salsa, it is always a good idea to cook the chicken along with part of the sauce.

- It is an excellent idea to line the bottom of the crockpot with potato chunks. There are several reasons why this is a beautiful idea. To begin, this method immediately converts any chicken meal into a one-pot supper option. In addition, you can be confident that the potato side dish will burst with flavor due to the chicken's fat and liquids absorbed by the potatoes. You can be sure that this will occur. It's a victory at dinnertime for everyone involved.

- Any crockpot dish would benefit tremendously from adding an acidic ingredient, like lemon juice. If you want to give your chicken dinner a little extra pop to brighten the flavor, save the squeeze of lemon for the end of the cooking process so that it stands out and doesn't get muted. This is especially important if you want to give your chicken meal a little pop to freshen the flavor.

- On the other hand, if you want to create lemon chicken or give your standard crockpot shredded chicken some flavor, go ahead and toss in the juice from a couple of lemons at the beginning of the cooking process. This will allow you to achieve either of these goals. It also enables the chicken to soak in a significant amount of the dish's flavor without absorbing much of the acidity.

18.3 Tips & Tricks on How to Keep the Meat from Getting Tough

Your crockpot has the potential to produce a roast that is so tender that it falls apart or a dinner that is rough, dry, and inedible. You must be aware of the responses to these questions. Are you using the appropriate kind of meat in this dish? Where do we stand about the ideal temperature? Are there sufficient amounts of liquid in the crockpot? Several aspects contribute to the overall quality of your food. Here is everything you need to prepare soft beef in a crockpot, as well as how to rectify things if the dish doesn't go as planned.

- The slow cooker's most flavorful and tender results are achieved with fatty, well-cut pieces of beef. This may also refer to the meat that is still on the bone. In other words, you should avoid purchasing chicken breasts that have been stripped of their skin and bones.

- When purchasing beef, look for cuts such as brisket, chuck roast, and stew beef. Shoulder or ribs are good options for the pork. Thighs of chicken are recommended as the chicken cut to use in a crockpot. The fact that rougher cuts are often less costly means they are ideal for meals prepared on a limited budget.

- To maintain a moist atmosphere, the crockpot requires liquid, which may come from meat or vegetable stock, wine, or even plain water. It is unnecessary to completely cover the meat with liquid to cook it since the crockpot has a lid that keeps liquids within properly. All that is required is a cup or two.

- Add enough liquid to come up approximately one-third of the way on the meats in the crockpot if you want the meal to have a sauce or if you are creating a stew. This is the amount of liquid that should be added if you cook a stew. Because of this, the meat may be braised instead than boiled. Meat that has been boiled becomes tough.

- Check the dish every so often while it's cooking. However, do not raise the cover. When you do this, heat and moisture are allowed to escape, which puts the texture of the meat in danger.

- Put the meat you use in the crockpot on the bottom, where it will be closest to the element that provides the heat. After adding the remaining ingredients and liquids, turn the setting on your crockpot to low. Cooking will take between 6 and 9 hours, so plan accordingly. The connective tissue and fat in the flesh are broken down by the lengthy and slow braise, resulting in delightfully tender and moist meat.

- Why does the crockpot not soften the meat completely? This is because you have not allowed the collagen to degrade. Extend the time the food is allowed to cook, check to see that it has the appropriate amount of liquid, and continue monitoring it.

18.4 How to Make a Great Yogurt with the Crockpot?

Making yogurt in a crockpot is a terrific method since it does not require additional equipment. If you have a crockpot, you are well informed about how it may assist you when cooking. When you make yogurt at home, the versatility of the crockpot as a container that can simultaneously heat the milk and incubate the yogurt is another thing that will blow your mind. It couldn't be much easier to understand. It is an excellent method to save money and ultimately control the components of your food.

You'll need the following ingredients:

- 1/2 gallon of milk
- Yogurt culture

Follow these instructions to make yogurt:

- Adjust the crockpot's setting to low and pour in the milk.
- Maintain at low setting for two and a half hours. This will provide you with a sufficient amount of time for milk to reach the desired temperature.
- Let the milk cool in the crockpot with the cover on for about three hours, bringing the temperature down to 110 degrees.

- After three hours, pour one to two cups of the warmed milk into a bowl. To that milk, add the yogurt culture. Before adding yogurt culture, you must ensure that the milk's temperature is correct. If the temperature exceeds 110 degrees, you risk destroying the live yogurt cultures.
- Mix it well by whisking, and return the starter-milk mixture to the crockpot where it was initially stored together with the remaining milk.
- Put the lid back on the crockpot, then wrap a thick bath towel around the whole pot and secure it with a rubber band.
- Allow the yogurt to culture for about eight to ten hours or overnight.
- After the culture has developed, transfer the yogurt from the crock pot to glass quart jars and place them in the refrigerator.
- Before usage, it is recommended to place the mixture in the refrigerator for at least six hours.

18.5 Copycat Crockpot Recipes

1. Escarole with White Beans

Prep time: 15 minutes

Cook time: 4 hours

Servings: 2

Ingredients

- 1 tbsp of extra-virgin olive oil
- 1/2 lb of dried cannellini beans
- 1 small head escarole, chopped
- 2 cups of unsalted chicken broth
- ½ tsp of kosher salt
- 3 large cloves garlic, smashed & chopped
- 1 1/2 tsp of ground pepper
- 1/2 cup of grated pecorino cheese
- 1/2 lemon juice

Instructions

- Add everything except cheese and escarole to the crockpot.
- Cook at low for 4 hours.
- Add escarole and cheese. Mix well. Cook for some time.
- Serve hot.

Nutrients: Kcal 301, Fats: 8g, Total Carbs: 40g, Proteins: 19g

2. Buffalo Chicken Chili

Prep time: 15 minutes

Cook time: 4 hours

Servings: 2

Ingredients

- ½ lb of boneless, skinless chicken breast
- ½ medium onion, finely chopped
- ¼ cup of crumbled blue cheese
- ½ can of black beans, no-salt-added, rinsed
- ½ tsp of dried oregano
- ½ can of chickpeas, no-salt-added, rinsed
- 1 tbsp of extra-virgin olive oil
- ½ can of diced tomatoes, no-salt-added
- 1 cup of unsalted chicken broth
- ½ can of tomato sauce, no-salt-added
- ⅓ cup of Buffalo sauce
- ¼ tsp of garlic powder
- ¼ cup of sour cream

Instructions

- Add everything to the crockpot.
- Cook at low for 4 hours.

Nutrients: Kcal 319, Fats: 9g, Total Carbs: 34g, Proteins: 25g

3. Sun-Dried Tomato Gnocchi

Prep time: 10 minutes

Cook time: 3 hours 15 minutes

Servings: 2

Ingredients

- 2 cloves of garlic, grated
- 1 cup of vegetable broth, unsalted
- ¼ cup of chopped fresh basil
- ¼ cup of chopped sun-dried tomatoes
- ½ tsp of ground pepper
- ½ pack of potato gnocchi
- 1/3 pack of baby spinach
- 1 small squash, halved, seeded & cut
- Parmesan cheese, grated

Instructions

- Add everything except cheese to the crockpot.
- Cook at low for 4 hours.
- Add cheese and cook for some time.

Nutrients: Kcal 389, Fats: 12g, Total Carbs: 63g, Proteins: 10g

4. Farro Soup with Brussels & Bacon

Prep time: 40 minutes

Cook time: 45 minutes

Servings: 2

Ingredients

- ½ tsp of salt
- 1/2 bay leaf
- ½ tsp of ground pepper
- 2 center-cut bacon slices, cut into thin slices
- 1/2 tbsp of sherry vinegar
- 1 cup of chopped sweet onion
- ½ cup of pearled farro

- 1 cup of shredded Brussels sprouts
- 1 tbsp of extra-virgin olive oil
- 2 cups of chicken broth, lower-sodium
- 1/2 tsp of minced garlic
- ¼ cup of heavy cream
- 1 pack of sliced cremini mushrooms
- 1 tsp of fresh thyme leaves

Instructions

- Add everything to the crockpot.
- Cook at low for 45 minutes.

Nutrients: Kcal 263, Fats: 11g, Total Carbs: 30g, Proteins: 11g

5. Kale Stew

Prep time: 10 minutes

Cook time: 4 hours 25 minutes

Servings: 2

Ingredients

- 2 cloves garlic, minced
- ½ can of diced tomatoes, no-salt-added
- 1/2 lemon juice
- 3 ounces of turkey kielbasa, sliced
- ¼ tsp of ground cumin
- 2 small carrots, thinly sliced
- ½ tsp of dried oregano
- 2 medium potatoes, scrubbed & cubed
- 1 tbsp of tomato paste
- ½ medium onion, diced
- 1 tbsp of extra-virgin olive oil
- ½ tsp of smoked paprika
- 1 cup of chopped Tuscan kale
- ½ cup of chicken broth, low-sodium
- ¼ cup of finely chopped parsley

Instructions

- Add everything to the crockpot.
- Cook at low for 4 hours & 25 minutes.
- Serve and enjoy.

Nutrients: Kcal 238, Fats: 10g, Total Carbs: 27g, Proteins: 14g

18.6 Brief Guide to All the Crockpot Errors

When you use new kitchen equipment for the first time, there is always a learning curve; however, obtaining an error message may knock the wind out of your sails! If you follow these suggestions, you should have everything back up and running in no time.

Blinking Light

It means that the crockpot's lid is in the incorrect position. Make sure the lid is fully closed and in the position where it says "locked" by lining up the triangle on the crockpot's lid with the lock.

E1

It means that there has been a disconnect in the internal circuits. To fix it, contact the company's customer service.

E2

It means that the crockpot's unit is overheated, the internal sensor has been detached, and the current is inadequate. Try operating the crockpot with a different plug. Please turn off the power to the device, take out the inner pot, and wait for it to cool down.

E3

It means that the lid needed to be correctly closed and adequately sealed. If you get this error message when using one of the crockpot's settings, it means that the lid did not shut or seal properly. To find a solution, please follow these steps:

- Turn the steam release valve to point in the "Release" direction, then wait for the device to depressurize.

- Remove the lid and inspect the underside to ensure that the sealing gasket, a big rubber ring, is attached to the underside of the lid correctly.

- After removing the lid and letting part of the steam escape, if it seems as if the recipe may need more liquid, add some, combine the ingredients, and then replace the lid while making sure the steam release valve is in the "Seal" position.

- After unplugging the device for at least five seconds, re-insert the plug and re-program your pot's settings to start the cooking process.

E4

It means that the crockpot is already pressurized. This error is initiated when the crockpot tries to start a new cooking or pressurization cycle when it is already pressured. To find a solution, please follow these steps:

- Turn the steam release valve to point in the "Release" direction, then wait for the device to depressurize.

- After removing the cover and letting some of the steam escape, check your recipe to see if it needs more liquid. If it does, add some more liquid, mix the ingredients, and replace the lid.

- If you use a pressure setting, check that the "Seal" position is selected on the steam release valve. If you were attempting to utilize a setting that did not need pressure, the same valve should be set to the "Release" position.

- After unplugging the device for at least five seconds, re-insert the plug and re-program your crockpot's settings to start the cooking process.

E5

It means the valve is not in the correct position or the lid is not sealed. This error message will display when the lid or the SRV is misused.

- When utilizing the brown or sauté mode, you should notice that the lid should never be utilized at any time.

- To use the lid while the slow cook or yogurt settings are being processed, the SRV has to be set to the "Release" position, which is the open position.

- If you receive the E5 notification while using saute mode, remove the lid or correctly position the valve to "Release" and then unplug the unit for at least 5 seconds before plugging it back in and re-programming your settings to begin cooking again.

- If you continue to receive this notification while using any of these other settings, you will need to contact customer service.

E6

It means that the unit is overheated. If you get this code while cooking, it indicates that the crockpot could not create sufficient steam to fully pressurize itself. To find a solution, please follow these steps:

- Ensure that the SRV is in the "Seal" position by turning it to the closed position. If it is not in the correct position, rotate it so that it is, and then go to the next step, which is step 3, further down.

- If the valve is in the correct position, turn it to the "Release" position and wait for the unit to depressurize before proceeding with the next step. The next step is to take off the lid and inspect the underside of it to ensure that the sealing gasket, a big rubber ring, is attached to the underside of the lid correctly.

- Pour an additional cup of liquid into the crockpot, mix the items in the pot, and then reattach the lid while ensuring the valve is in the "Seal" position.

- After unplugging the device for at least five seconds, re-insert the plug and re-program your cook settings to start the cooking process.

-

18.7 Crockpot Safety Guidelines for Proper & Safe Use

Enjoy some tranquility while your supper is gently simmering away in the crockpot. The essential crockpot safety recommendations that you should know are discussed below. By a wide margin, one of our most prized possessions in the kitchen is the crockpot. What's not to adore about it? Because there are so many simple recipes, such as the best chili for the crockpot, you can just set it and forget it. The use of the crockpot to generate substantial meals that can be prepared in advance has become a popular cooking method throughout the autumn and winter months. However, similar to other types of electric cookware, a few potential safety hazards should be considered. If you need clarification on whether or not it's safe to use your crockpot, don't worry. Let's walk you through the proper procedures to cook without any anxiety.

- Cooking with a crockpot should be done conveniently on the countertop over an extended period. It is okay to leave it alone, even while cooking recipes that take 8 hours to complete, such as red beans and sausage. After twenty-four hours, most crockpots manufactured nowadays will turn themselves off automatically.

- Before leaving home, check to see that the appliance is turned down to a low setting, is moved away from any walls, and is put on a surface resistant to heat. If you follow these measures and plug them in overnight, you will quickly fall and stay asleep.

- If you are still using your old crockpot, now is the time to examine it. Check to see that the cables that come with the crockpot are in excellent shape. You should only use the appliance if the cable has frayed or is utterly intact from the device to the socket. Get rid of it immediately if it has begun to give off an odd odor.

- Putting a frozen dish straight into the crockpot may be tempting, but you should resist the urge. As the FDA recommends, it is much safer to let frozen meat defrost before cooking it. When defrosting a prepared frozen item, follow the precise directions that come with the box.

- Every single one of your crockpot recipes must have some liquid foundation. This prevents the components from being overheated, which would cause them to adhere to the bottom of the dish and maybe catch fire. In soups like vegetarian lentils, liquids like broth may provide a significant flavor while also helping maintain the meal's moisture and tenderness.

- You should never load your crockpot more than two-thirds of the way up, even though it may be tempting to pack as much as possible. When anything is overfilled, it increases the risk of spills, messes, and food that is not fully cooked. Before utilizing, it is essential to check the owner's handbook of your appliance to determine its maximum capacity in terms of volume.

- Cutting your meat into smaller portions may reduce the time it takes to cook and make it simpler to incorporate other ingredients into the meal. This is true even if it is perfectly safe to cook vast pieces of meat, such as in the crockpot roast chicken recipe. Please refer to the instructions in your crock pot's instruction manual for more advice.

  - Refrain from looking into the crockpot while cooking, even though it is pretty tempting. When the cover is taken off, it allows the heat accumulating within the dish to escape. This may cause the cooking procedure to take longer.

- As an additional safety measure, fire departments suggest you unplug your home equipment whenever it is not in use. The "off" button is not sufficient protection for your crockpot; thus, the next time you are through using it, disconnect it and put it away in a secure location.

Conclusion

The crockpot is an excellent kitchen appliance. Even if you know nothing about crockpots, this book will help you through it all. It's a complete guide for novice people who want to make daily life easier and less hectic. After reading this book, you know all about the crockpot's features, settings and other options. Now you know what to cook and how to cook. You can choose a crockpot according to your preference. This book has also enabled you to keep your appliance safe and clean by following the methods mentioned. It has given you all the tips and tricks that will help you make delicious meals in a crockpot.

It's time to switch up your weekly menu with exciting new crockpot recipes; getting this book is the perfect opportunity. They are a blessing at those times when one is pressed for time. These straightforward recipes for the crockpot will teach you how to get the most out of this versatile kitchen gadget, whether you've had one for years or are just now learning about its many benefits.

This cookbook provides a wide variety of mouthwatering crockpot recipes for you and your loved ones. Explicit directions for each stage of the cooking process are given. Each recipe includes a detailed list of the ingredients, the amount of time needed for preparation, an exact cooking time and temperature, serving advice, and other nutritional data, among other things. This cookbook offers a lot of images to share with you so you can get a better idea of what the meal looks like.

A well-thought-out meal plan should serve as the foundation for developing healthy eating routines. Utilizing the meal plan in this cookbook will assist you in developing healthy eating routines.

Precisely what are you going to be looking forward to? Why go somewhere else when you can get all the necessary information, including a comprehensive and step-by-step guide on preparing those delicious things in your crockpot, right here? Now that you have all the required information, start cooking in your crockpot.

Recipe Index

W

Y

Z

Printed in Great Britain
by Amazon

19054096R00095